"GET IT TOGETHER" — TOGETHER!

"GET IT TOGETHER" — TOGETHER!

by

Dennis Delisle

"Get It Together" — Together!
ISBN 0-927936-60-7
Copyright © 1994 by Dennis Delisle
5328 South Monterey Hwy., Suite B
San Jose, CA 95111
(408) 226-6100

Published by
VINCOM, Inc.
P. O. Box 702400
Tulsa, OK 74170
(918) 254-1276

Dedication

I dedicate this book to my wife, Sharon, for all she has done to make my life and family so special. She certainly is a Proverbs 31 lady.

To my daughter, Annette, who is such a precious young lady. God has anointed her with a special mission to help people.

To my son, Dennis, Jr., whose wonderful temperament can relate to cowboys riding bulls as well as being an executive and running our business operations.

Contents

Acknowledgements

Foreword by Dexter R. Yager, Sr.

Preface

Acknowledgements

Have you ever started something and quit when the challenges got too big? Your heart says "yes," but circumstances seem to say "no." The fear of failure creeps in. We've all been there.

In my heart, I wanted to share some principles that I believe will help parents in rearing children and help husbands and wives in their relationships. After a couple of years of writing this book, I finally gave up on this dream until, through our good friends, Mark and Sandy Day, we met and built a friendship with Randal and Andrea Ross. I want to thank them for their help in putting this book together and their chapter contributions. Without them, this dream could have died!

I would also like to thank Larry Keefauver for writing much of the Bible study sections, and George Vinnett, my publisher, for his enthusiasm and help with the book.

Finally, I would like to thank my son Dennis Jr. and my nephew Ricky Delisle for the concept of the cover of my book.

Foreword

by Dexter R. Yager, Sr.

Often, when reading a book, we take a passive role. We sit comfortably in our den and mindlessly turn the pages. This book is definitely not like that! *Get It Together - Together* is a powerful book which can really change the lives of those who will use it as it is intended to be used. It is really a hands-on tool to help re-establish families in America. I believe that if families will spend time together, truly studying this book, along with their Bibles, we would see America getting back on track with strong family values.

The Delisles' are a wonderful family. Dennis and Sharon have been married for almost twenty-seven years, and they have two great children. Most people who see them believe they are the "perfect" family, and they are. Like all good things, though, their strong family unity has not happened by chance. They work on it daily.

I remember back when Birdie and I were living in New York with our kids. We had seven children while we were still in our twenties. In a family that size, there is constant competition. Kids fighting for the bathroom, fighting for attention, or even the last piece of fried chicken! One thing we had to learn very quickly was to teach our kids not to be overly competitive with each other. Each child was different, with different talents, so we learned to cultivate those talents. Jeff was always very good with numbers, so as he grew, we put him in charge of our finances. Doyle is very creative, and today he is responsible for most of the new tools which Internet carries. Steven is a very organized person, and he's great with people. Today he manages our warehouse operation with over forty employees. We all need to use the talents we were given and teach our children to do the same.

Children are a blessing from God, and one of the most important things we can do for our kids is help build their self-esteem. Give them encouragement. Birdie and I have always been tough with our kids, but they've always known they were loved. We've never offered them a free ride, but we have shown them how to set goals and work to achieve them. A child will value that new car much more if they work hard and earn it for themselves. Don't cheat your children out of the satisfaction of being able to say, "I did it!"

As Dennis says, "Life is a growth process of getting your life together," and the first step to getting it all together is getting right with God. Get your relationship right with God first, and the other areas of your life will follow. Once we have affirmed our relationship with God, then we can begin to work on relationships with our husband or wife, our children and even our finances.

As this book will teach you, one of the first steps to getting it together is to have husband and wife Bible studies. Marriage is a partnership, with the husband as the leader. We should honor and appreciate our husband or wife and tell them every day how much we love them.

We will always be faced with challenges. It is not the challenge that is important but how we handle it. The Bible teaches us to pray without ceasing. When something bad comes your way, don't spend time and energy worrying about it — pray about it. Every night before you go to bed, turn all your worries over to God. He's going to be up all night anyway!!

Even if we do everything that is taught in this book, life will never be "perfect." God made us human, so there will always be some type of failure in our lives. When you experience a failure, get over it and move on. Don't let your past be a roadblock to your future. We've all heard the phrase, "Quitters never win," and I'm a firm believer in that.

One thing that will help you as you get it all together is for you to fill your mind with godly, positive material. Close your eyes for thirty seconds, and try to think about absolutely nothing. You can't do it. It is not possible. No matter how hard you try, your mind will always be active. Fill your mind with godly things, and when your mind wanders, bring it back and focus on what is good.

This book can help you maintain that positive focus. Read it daily, along with your Bible, with your husband or wife. Complete all the worksheets following each chapter, and really study and dwell on what it teaches. It *will* help you *Get It Together — Together.*

Preface

Why this book? My prayer is that it will help you *Get It Together - Together* — to help you realize that we were made to worship a wonderful Creator, and to know that no life can be truly happy or joyous without the relationship with the Father that only comes through the Son. This book will help you get it together with your spouse, your children and your centers of influence. My goal is for families to start studying the Bible together. It will help you grow individually and then you will be blessed to watch the tremendous growth in your family.

The idea of a family or husband and wife Bible study came to me after my wife, Sharon, and I tried to do a husband and wife study together. We got into our most serious fight in our lives. Crazy! It made me realize that we needed a simplified Bible study in the marketplace. But it also made me realize how vital communication through Bible study is for everyone.

I know that men are not as open as women. Inside, we would like to let go and drop our "walls of protection," but it is really scary for men. The Bible study is a great way to start lowering those walls one brick at a time. I would encourage the men to take the leadership role in the home and get started. God will give you the wisdom to help draw your whole family toward Him.

1

"Get It Together" — God

By Randal Ross

Congratulations! You have just made the single most significant decision anyone could ever make to get their life together. It is the decision to get your life together with God's help.

Life's greatest miracles come when we are honest with ourselves and make the big decision to turn our lives around and start over. The question now is: "How do we get our lives together?"

I remember all the times I was going to get it together, but I didn't know how to do it or where to start. This book is designed to help you know with whom you are to get it together and how to get it together. You will learn from those who have had the same questions and challenges you have experienced, and from those who have discovered the joy of getting life together. You can do it! It's not too late, and it's not too hard!

Do you remember Humpty Dumpty? He sat on the wall and had a great fall, and all the king's horses and all the king's men couldn't put Humpty Dumpty together again. His life was hopelessly broken and no one could help him. The good news is, you're not Humpty Dumpty! You *can* get the pieces back together again and experience a "together life." No matter how shattered, broken or sinful your life has been, God can fix it!

Where do we begin? Getting it together has to begin with God. He holds the key to getting life together. He is the One Who made you and designed a plan for your life. If you want to get your life together and rebuild it, you will have to learn to get together with God.

I'm sure that sounds frightening to some, impossible to others, or even unnecessary. However, the truth is, *you can rise no higher in life than your understanding of God and your relationship with Him.* Let me explain why this is so important.

Many of life's problems come from a warped view of God. What is a damaged or warped view of God? Let's say you believe He is out to hurt you or take from you rather than add to your life. If this is your view, then you will live in constant fear that He will do exactly that. It would be like running a race with a bowling ball around your neck. Life would become a drag. You would always be trying to keep God off your back rather than asking Him to help and lead you into a better, more complete life.

I have good news for you! God is not against you. He does not hate you, nor is He out to hurt you. The truth is, God loves you like no one else in the universe. He loves you just as you are. It doesn't matter what you have done in the past. He loves you and wants to help you put your life together again.

How do we know that God really loves us and is for us? We know this because He said so and He cannot lie. In John 3:16-17, Jesus tells us these eternal words:

> **For God so loved the world that he gave his one and only Son, that whoever believes in him shall not perish but have eternal life.**

> **For God did not send his Son into the world to condemn the world, but to save the world through him.**

God openly says He loves you. He has proven His love for you by sending His Son, Jesus Christ, to die for you so you can get it together with the heavenly Father.

God understands you, and He created you to find happiness through an intimate, personal relationship with Jesus Christ. That's right! God loves you just like you are and right where you are. He will never love you more than He loves you right now. As you have probably discovered, life without Christ at the helm of it just doesn't work. There is a great price to pay to live your life without Christ.

If you are like me, you might have a hard time believing that God is for you and that He loves you. But once you get a hold of this concept, it will change the way you see yourself and others.

Christianity is really very simple. Even a young child can live for God and enjoy His presence and power. But Christianity is not easy. It requires a new way of thinking and a new way of living.

You will find yourself making a few mistakes (maybe even lots of them)! There are many temptations set to get you off track and to cause you to lose your perspective. Christianity is a journey. You never stop growing in Christ. You never "arrive" in this life. There are no perfect people — just those who have committed their lives to Christ and are committed to walk with Him. Even committed Christians have challenges "talking the talk" and "walking the walk." The good news is, even when we fail, God still loves us.

Several key principles will enable you to get it together with God. I will share them with you, but first, it is important that you know the two big themes of Christianity — God's two big ideas.

• *Christianity is not you living for God, but it is God living in you!*

For years I wanted to serve God and even made commitments to be a good Christian, but I could never keep those promises. I would say things like, "I'm so sorry for my failures and sins. I'm going to be better. I am going to stop doing bad things and start doing good things." I really meant it.

The trouble was, I could not keep my promises. I felt like such a failure that I quit trying and quit promising.

One day I learned what Christianity really is. It is a step of faith, or trusting Jesus to do for me what I could not do for myself. I discovered the wonderful truth that Christianity is not about my promises and abilities, but it's about letting Jesus live inside of my heart — receiving Him as Savior and Lord.

I said, "Lord, I can't be better in my own power, but I want You to live in me." When Jesus came into my heart, He changed me. Suddenly, it was Christ living in me, giving me the ability, desire and perspective I needed. What a difference it made in my life. That step of faith will do the same for you.

The Bible says, **Yet to all who received him, to those who believed in his name, he gave the right to become children of God** (John 1:12).

Remember, Christianity is not about your ability. It is about God's life coming into you and living through you!

• *Christianity is a relationship, not just an event or a decision.*

God is not an idea, an emotion, or a theology. You relate to Him just as you do to other people. He wants to talk to you. He wants to love you and hear that you love Him. Being a Christian is like getting married. You make a decision and walk down the aisle, but then you learn to relate to your partner.

The longer you serve God and the more you know about Him, the better your relationship becomes. Living with Jesus in an intimate, personal way is the best thing that can ever happen in your life. Guaranteed! God wants an intimate, personal relationship with you, not just a passing moment in a time of crisis or need. Let me explain this truth through a personal story.

When I was a young boy, I had a hero. His name was John F. Kennedy, the President of the United States. He was everything I wanted to be — handsome, rich, famous and married to a beautiful lady. One day I heard that President Kennedy was going to come through our little town in Ohio. I was so excited. I begged my parents to let me go and stand on the street to see and meet my hero.

I showed up hours early and waited. Then it happened. His black convertible turned the corner and began coming toward me. He was waving and everyone was cheering. I was determined to shake his hand. As his car passed by me, I made my move. I rushed out and shook his hand. I wanted to hold on, but the police pushed me back. He smiled at me and then he was gone.

As I looked down at my hand, I thought to myself, "This is the hand that touched the hand of President Kennedy." Then my mind began building it up, and I started telling everyone that not only had I met President Kennedy, but he was my friend. We were going to get together and talk. The more I bragged, the bigger the illusion got. I even started believing it myself. But the truth is, I did not have a personal relationship with the President. I had met him only in a moment. Then I went on my way.

This is how some people see Christianity. They think it is a moment of touching Jesus, a moment of decision, or a crisis call for help. True Christianity is more. It is a personal, abiding relationship with God, in touch with Him, growing closer to Him through prayer and meditating in His Word daily.

Do you know Jesus personally? The most important thing in life is to know Christ. If you do not have a personal relationship with Him, you can right now. Just stop a moment and ask Christ to come into your life.

Be honest! Tell Him your failures and your fears. Then receive Him as your Savior, and He will live inside of you! Now you're on the right track. You are His child. You are forgiven and on your way to a wonderful new life with God! Now, let's take a look at the keys to getting it together with Him.

The first key to getting it together with God is to learn to live your life by FAITH.

The world's system of belief is based on seeing and then believing. It is just the opposite in God's Kingdom. First, you believe and then you see. It sounds upside down, but it is called faith. Faith is the key that releases the power and the blessings of God into your life (see Heb. 11:1-3; Eph. 2:8; Rom. 5:2; and Matt. 17:20).

How can we believe and act on something we have not seen? We do this by trusting God's character. Faith is not a mind game where we pump ourselves up to go against reality. It is trusting the character of God. He is good, true and faithful. That means you can act on the promises of His Word because He will perform it in your behalf (Jer. 1:12). He will not let you down. The power of Christianity is that if we trust, obey and become doers of His Word, then *God will always do His part.*

That makes Christianity an ever-growing adventure. As you grow more in trusting God's character and His Word, you will find more of His blessings in your life. You will become more confident in the difficult situations where it may look like failure, but God will come through for you just as He has promised.

Learn to grow daily in the life of *faith.* How do we grow in faith? We grow by reading His Word and doing what He tells us to do, which is called **obedience**.

Obedience is often very hard for us Americans because we are used to doing things our own way. Obedience leads us to spiritual growth and helps us to avoid unnecessary hardships in our lives.

I can point to a hundred times where God's Word told me not to do something, but I did it anyway. Later, I found out that God was right all along! Now that I am learning to ask God first and then follow Him and obey in faith, the results are so much better. Faith is the first key to getting it together with God.

The second key to getting it together with God is learning to LOVE.

Love is the greatest and most important part of Christianity. Jesus said you can always tell the false people from the real ones by their commitment to Him and to the presence of real love in their lives. He said, **By this all men will know that you are my disciples, if you love one another** (John 13:35).

What does it mean to love? It means to put others ahead of yourself. We are to love God first. That means we are to want His will and His pleasure more than anything else. God does not just want our minds or acts of service. He wants our hearts, just as you want those who matter in your life to love and obey you. Christianity is a matter of the heart, not just the head.

Love means that we are to treat others as we want to be treated. It is best expressed in forgiveness. Jesus makes it very clear that we are to forgive others as He has forgiven us, or our spiritual lives will be greatly hindered.

> **And when you stand praying, if you hold anything against anyone, forgive him, so that your Father in heaven may forgive you your sins.**
> **Mark 11:25**

Every person has a prison on the inside where they keep those who have hurt or harmed them. We keep them there, withholding love to them until they have paid. We must let others go from our "inner prisons." Jesus said if you let them go, bless them and love them, He will let your pain and failures go, too. That can be very hard to do if you have been deeply wounded by others. You must keep your eyes on Jesus and look at the great love He has shown by forgiving you. Then give that gift of freedom to others.

We must also learn to love ourselves. That can sound terribly unspiritual, but I assure you, it is God's will for your life. Jesus told us we are to love God first and then others just as we love ourselves.

It is hard to love others if we don't love ourselves. How can we love ourselves? Easy! We love ourselves by accepting that God loves us and that He gives us value. If He so loved us and thought we were important enough to die for us, then we should accept His opinion of us and live our lives as important and valuable individuals.

You can know that you really have a Biblical self-image when you believe God truly values you. And you, in turn, give that value to others.

The third key to getting it together with God is DISCIPLE-SHIP. God has not just called you to be a Christian but to be a **disciple** of Christ. A disciple is a learner, someone who is dedicated to growing in knowledge and understanding of truth. A disciple is one who grows more and more in the likeness of his teacher and leader. That means that as a believer in Christ, we are to grow more and more in His character and purpose.

God has a purpose for your life. What is that purpose? It is to bring Him honor and glory as you grow and achieve His will for your life. His purpose is for you to be His messenger of love and forgiveness to others. You are not on this earth at this time by accident or only to survive, pay the bills and retire. You are here for a reason. When you find that reason, your whole life will become exciting, challenging and adventurous. It is then that you will really start to live.

How do we become disciples? We do this through regular Bible study, prayer and ministry. The Bible is our textbook. It holds the keys to all of life. Believe me, it is the most wonderful, relevant book ever written. It is God's message to you. Find a translation that is easy for you to understand and begin to read it daily. I suggest the *New International Version* or the *New King James Version*. As a Christian, you need to become part of a regular Bible study. (One of the purposes of this book is to get you started in a family Bible study.)

Something wonderful happens when you study God's Word together with others. It comes alive. You will see new truths, and it will become easier to apply God's truths to your life. It is vital that you find a local church where you can belong and hear Biblical, encouraging and challenging messages. It would also be beneficial to you to attend Sunday school and a neighborhood or business Bible study if one is available.

Just as Bible study is important, you need to pray every day. It's not hard to pray. Just talk with God in your own language. Tell Him what is going on in your life. Ask for His help and then listen for His answers.

Any of the following books will help you pray more effectively:

Power Through Prayer by E. M. Bounds.

Warfare Prayer by Peter Wagner.

Prayer: A Holy Occupation by Oswald Chambers.

Prayer by Frank Leubach.

Power and Peace in Prayer by R. A. Torrey.

Finally, a disciple is one who gives to others. God has a purpose and a ministry for you to fulfill. Christianity is not just you growing in Christ, but you helping others find Christ and making their lives better. God asks us to give of our time, talents and resources to others. You found Christ because someone shared with you. Now it is your turn to share Him with others.

Part of discipleship is giving of your finances. God promises to bless you financially as you trust Him with your money. Give of your talents. Use the gifts God has given you. Give of your time. When we help others in simple ways, God calls us faithful servants and He blesses us. Service to others causes Christianity to come alive, and it keeps us from becoming self-centered and hard-hearted.

The fourth key to getting it together with God is FELLOW-SHIP. You do not serve God alone. You are part of a wonderful family called the family of God. God never intended for you to serve Him or find fulfillment alone, but it is His plan that you join your life with others of like faith.

It is important that you identify with other Christians. To worship God together is not only God's command, but it provides a wonderful lifting of our lives into God's very presence. What better place to start than with a family fellowship. Jesus promised to be with us always, but He also promised to be with us in a special way when we get together!

Being a Christian is rarely easy. We need others in our lives who can mentor, encourage and help us grow spiritually. In the Body of Christ, there are people who have gifts and abilities to help us in our weak areas. We, in turn, find others who need exactly what we have to offer. Jesus told us not to stop meeting together. We are to make a point of having fellowship with other Christians. After all, we will spend eternity together, so why not start now?

Finally, Christ has called us to share our faith. We are given a great commission — to share Jesus Christ with a world that does not know Him. As a Christian, you are God's ambassador, His messenger. Learn to share your faith with others. Leading others to Christ is one of life's greatest blessings. It really isn't that hard. You just need to know a few scriptures and then tell your story. Tell others the difference Jesus has made in your life. Tell them God loves them and wants them to love Him and others. Together we can change the world.

It might sound a little overwhelming, but really, it all just flows together as you fall in love with Jesus. Remember, don't make it harder than it is! It is Christ living in you that makes the difference. It is a relationship with Him, so keep in constant contact with Him. There are others who can help you when you get stuck or discouraged. Don't give up! You can do all things God has called you to do through Christ! He has already made you a winner!

I am praying for you, and I believe in you! Please complete the following Bible Study which will help you get started in getting it together with God!

I would like to take this opportunity at the close of Randal's chapter to thank the men in my life who have helped me break down the walls of logic and skepticism. These men have been a vital influence in my life.

Frank Delisle, Sr.	My dad always took our family to church each Sunday.
Rich DeVos	Rich first encouraged me to read my Bible and work to understand what God was saying to me and to grow in my spiritual walk.
Frank Delisle, Jr.	My brother is such an encouragement to me and is uplifting to all who come in contact with him.
Charlie Youngkin	My pastor from Morgan Hill Bible Church who is always available to interpret and teach from Scripture.
Mark Day	Mark touched my life as a young man following God's plan for his life.
Randal Ross	A preacher who is a man's man. Tough, yet surrendered to Christ.
Dexter Yager	A modern-day hero every father would want his sons to follow. He is a success in all areas of his life, and he motivates me to become better in all that I do.

I encourage men to find mentors in their lives who are sold out to Christ. These role models will help you to become better.

Dennis P. Delisle

Bible Study

INSTRUCTIONS: Be honest with yourself as you complete this study. If you are studying in a group or with your family, share those things you feel most comfortable in sharing. Do one question each day for the next week, or spend thirty minutes completing the entire study at one time.

For Couples:

1. Share with one another the first time you knew for sure that you had a personal relationship with Jesus Christ as your Lord and Savior.

   - How old were you and where were you?

   - What person or persons were most instrumental in sharing Jesus with you?

   - What was the greatest obstacle you faced in accepting Jesus?

2. How do you feel about loving yourself?

   - What five things do you love about yourself?

     a. _____

     b. _____

     c. _____

     d. _____

     e. _____

   - What five things do you love about your spouse?

     a. _____

     b. _____

     c. _____

     d. _____

     e. _____

- When is it hardest to tell your spouse that you love him/her? When is it easiest?

3. Write your own definition of *faith*. _____

   _____

   _____

   Now read Hebrews 11:1-3. In your own words, write the definition of faith found in these verses. _____

   _____

   _____

   _____

4. Share with one another your definitions of *trust* or *faith*. Your definition of *disciple*.

5. Say to one another, **"I am a disciple of Jesus Christ."** Explain to one another what that means.

6. Complete these sentences for one another.

   God's purpose for my life is _____

   The one thing I need from God right now is _____

   The one thing I need from you right now is _____

   My greatest fear is _____

   My greatest joy is_____

   My greatest hope is _____

7. Read Matthew 22:37-39. List the ways given in these verses that you can show your love.

   To God: _____

   _____

   To others: _____

   _____

   To yourself: _____

   _____

When was the last time you told another person you loved them? _____

When was the last time you told God you loved Him?

_____

For Parents and Children...

1. Share with one another:

   • I trust in Jesus because _____

2. Each of you draw a picture of your family around the dinner table. Share what you like best and least about family dinner times.

(Use crayons or colored markers, if available.)

3. Do a trust walk with each other. Take turns being blind-folded, and the one without the blindfold leading the blindfolded one around. After doing this share:
   - What did you feel when you were blindfolded?
   - How is this like faith?

4. Sit facing one another. The parent will go first and share one minute of things they like and appreciate about their child. Then the child will share things they like about their parents.

     Give each other a hug and pray for one another like this:

     "Jesus, I thank You for _____(name)_____. Amen."

2

"Get It Together" — Yourself

Forget the former things; do not dwell on the past.

See, I am doing a new thing! Now it springs up; do you not perceive it?

Isaiah 43:18,19

Your past is over. To get along with yourself, you need to deal with it and let it go.

Often, people who come from a broken home or an alcoholic or abusive past, use it as a cop-out to excuse their own behavior: "That's the way I am because of my environment. It's my family's fault. It's not my fault."

Though your past may not have been good, at a certain age you become accountable where you can make a choice to change your future. To keep dwelling on your past will hinder where you are going. God has given us the innate ability to overcome the worst memories of our past, no matter how bad, and literally determine the destiny of our own lives.

Every person must understand that they are created in God's likeness and image. God is so concerned about each person that in Isaiah 49:16 He said, **See, I have engraved you on the palms of my hands.** He says in Jeremiah 29:11, **"For I know the plans I have for you," declares the Lord, "plans to prosper you and not to harm you, plans to give you hope and a future."**

Some of the steps to overcome your past are:

1. *Change your thinking.* Most people who aren't "accomplishers" think of bad instead of good. They think of what is wrong instead of what is right. A good example is a person might say, "This glass is half empty," instead of "This glass is half full."

2. *Change your input.* Turn off the TV and the radio and open a self-help book. There are plenty of great books on the market today on relationships, personal growth, goal-setting and becoming the person you want to be. One such book is *Seven Habits of Winning Relationships* by Randal Ross.

3. *Change your associations.* You can't hang around with losers and be a winner. Choose your friends. When you make a choice to change your life, some people will try to pull you down. Hang around with people who do share your ideas, dreams and convictions.

For example, if you are hanging around with the bar group who wants to go out and party all the time, you are not going to have a great family life because you're in a wrong environment. Wrong actions produce wrong results.

4. *Act like you are a success, even though you might not feel like it.* Act like the person you want to be.

Second Corinthians 5:17 says, **Therefore, if anyone is in Christ, he is a new creation; the old has gone, the new has come!** Philippians 4:13 says, **I can do everything through him who gives me strength.**

5. *You are a unique person.* God created every person special. Therefore, don't use other people to determine your self-worth, because people will often let you down. Choose God as your source of identity, and base your life on His approval.

Psalm 139:13-18 says:

> **For you created my inmost being; you knit me together in my mother's womb.**

> I praise you because I am fearfully and wonderfully made; your works are wonderful, and I know that full well.
>
> My frame was not hidden from you when I was made in the secret place. When I was woven together in the depths of the earth,
>
> Your eyes saw my unformed body. All the days ordained for me were written in your book before one of them came to be.
>
> How precious to me are your thoughts, O God! How vast is the sum of them!
>
> Were I to count them, they would outnumber the grains of sand. When I awake, I am still with you.

Once you decide to base your life on God's approval, you will begin to like yourself for who you are.

6. *Be patient with yourself.* Give yourself realistic time-tables. Don't get discouraged when you make a mistake. Part of your growth will come from making mistakes. You aren't going to succeed at everything you do.

In learning to bowl, for example, when you throw a gutter ball, it's a long way back to your seat. When you throw a strike, it's easy to go back and sit down. If you never threw a gutter ball, you would never know how to throw a strike. The process of learning to bowl includes knowing how to hold the ball, how to throw the ball and how to get it down the middle of the lane.

Similarly, in your personal growth process, you will occasionally fail. Instead of saying, "I failed at what I was trying to accomplish," you should say, "I am going to get better next time, and I will not make the same mistake again."

7. *Allow yourself some personal renewal time.* Identify the things that bring renewal to you. For a young mother, this can mean an hour or two break to read, shop, or just be by herself. For some people, it is playing tennis, racquet ball, or a round of golf. For others it may be going for a swim or just spending some quiet time alone.

8. *Learn to laugh at yourself and with others.* When you take life too seriously, you will take all the joy out of the moments with your mate and with your children. After all, Proverbs 17:22a says, **A cheerful heart is good medicine.**

Some of the challenges, pains, or hurts you experience will build and solidify the foundation of your life. People tend to think that once you become successful, wealthy, or achieve fame, all your problems are over. The truth is, you just get a whole new set of problems. So if you don't learn how to handle the smaller problems, you'll never learn how to handle the bigger ones.

Romans 5:3,4 says:

> **We also rejoice in our sufferings, because we know that suffering produces perseverance;**
>
> **Perseverance, character; and character, hope.**

9. *It's okay to feel good about yourself.* Some Christians have been taught that feeling good about themselves is bad, but God wants us to feel good about ourselves. It is okay to enjoy life, to feel good when you do something right like hitting a home run! It's okay to laugh and run the bases and take a high five because that's the way God made us to be. You don't have to be down on yourself to be spiritual. God wants you to be up! He wants you to succeed in what He has called you to do.

You need to realize, it's okay to get along with yourself. You don't have to fight yourself to please God. The more you feel good about yourself, the easier it is for you to feel good about other people.

10. *Failure isn't permanent.* You can learn from failure, grow from it, get up and go forward.

Personal growth is a life journey, not a destination. Life is to be lived until the end. If you stay hungry to grow, learn and improve, you can live life fully to the end. Never think that because you are 40, 50, 80, or even 90 that your life is over. Some of the greatest discoveries and contributions to life have been made during a person's later years.

You need to have a goal or a purpose in life to really like yourself. God made Adam and Eve to till the garden, name the animals and manage the property for God.

If you are going to like yourself, you can't stay idle. You need to have a goal and work toward something you don't have right now to have a sense of accomplishment that makes you feel good about yourself.

When you quit existing for a purpose, you become self-centered. People begin to deteriorate when they have no dreams or goals. Old age is a state of mind.

God made us to be givers in this world's system — to accomplish something and help others along the way. As we do that, we will make others happy, and we will also begin to like ourselves better.

Luke 6:38 says, **Give, and it will be given to you. A good measure, pressed down, shaken together and running over, will be poured into your lap. For with the measure you use, it will be measured to you.**

The principle of giving to others is applicable, not just before age 65, but all through life. I know some people who are in their mid-80s and early 90s who are still giving and refuse to stop. They have kept their health and strength, and they are exciting to be around.

Most people think, "How could I squeeze anything else into my life?" Many people's lives are without goals. Either they don't have a goal they really want to accomplish, or their goal is to get to work, get back home, turn on the TV and have a beer. If you have a dream, a goal, or a purpose, your life becomes more focused and efficient. You actually have time to accomplish more.

Happiness and self-esteem don't come from leisure alone. They come from doing what God has called each of us to do.

When Sharon and I first started our business together, our dream was to build a business so we would be able to retire at a certain age. But as we became more successful, we realized that success is a process. In this process, you set new goals that inspire, serve and fulfill your lives while being involved in other people's lives. To retire means to get away from something. In life we are always called to be servants of Christ. Nowhere in Scripture does it give you an age of retirement. It shows you how your emphasis changes from working to instruction of others of what you have learned best.

Bible Study

INSTRUCTIONS: Be honest with yourself as you complete this study. If you are studying in a group or with your family, share those things you feel most comfortable in sharing. Do one question each day for the next week, or spend thirty minutes completing the entire study at one time.

For Couples...

1. Each of you, alone at first, think of a time in your marriage that was most exciting for you. Then think of a time that was most traumatic for you. As a couple, share together:

   • One of the most exciting times in our marriage for me was....

   • One of the most traumatic times in our marriage was....

2. As a couple, pray this prayer in unison:

   "Heavenly Father, thank You for seeing us through the trauma in the past. Through Your Holy Spirit, give us the power to let go of the past and to receive the new things You are doing in our lives and marriage, in Jesus' name. Amen."

3. As a couple, share what you each feel is the most exciting thing that God is doing:

   • In your marriage

   • In your family

   • In your work

   • In your spiritual lives

   There are certain steps to overcoming the past. In order to overcome the past, what will you do? Complete each of the following sentences:

   • One way of thinking I will change is_____

- One source of input I will change is_____
- One association I need to change is _____
- One feeling I have that needs to change is_____
- One way I need to be patient with myself is_____
- One way to have more personal renewal time is_____

4. Share something on your list with your marriage partner.

5. Now share with one another something humorous that has happened to you in the past week, and then pray together, thanking God for the ways that He has given you to be set free from your past.

6. Read 2 Corinthians 5:17. When you are born again, Paul says you are "in Christ." According to Paul, what do you then become?

   _____

   When you are born again, what happens to your "old life"?

   _____

7. Psalm 139:19 says you are _____and _____ made.

8. Proverbs 17:22a says a _____ _____ is as medicine to your entire being.

   Are you taking this medicine each day?
   _____ Yes   _____ No

   Is there an adjustment you need to make to increase this flow of medicine?

   _____ Yes   _____ No

For Families...

1. As a family, go around to each person in the family and share one funny thing that stands out in your memory about something that happened in your family's past.

2. After everyone has shared a funny time from the past, go around again and ask each person to share, "The greatest learning experience I ever had in the family was...."

   _____

   _____

3. From the oldest person to the youngest person in the family, you are now going to go around the table and have everyone focus on each person in the family while reading in unison the following scripture to that person out loud. When you get to the blank, insert that person's name so that when you have finished, every person in the circle will have heard this passage read in a personal way to them.

   "See, I [the Lord] **have engraved** _____
   upon the palms of My hands...for I know the plans I
   [the Lord] **have for** _____**, plans**
   to prosper_____ **and not to harm**
   _____**, plans to give**
   _____ **hope and a future"**
   (Isa. 49:16; Jer. 29:11).

4. As a family, look at the steps listed in chapter 2 for overcoming the past, and each of you choose one step that you need to take in the coming week that will help you more effectively overcome the past. Share with each one in your family which step you have chosen and something about why you chose that step. Pray in a circle together as a family for one another to take that step that needs to be taken. For example, "Lord, I pray that John can take the step he needs to take to change his input for this next week. Amen."

3
"Get It Together" — Wife

To build up your wife is to build your own life. In case you haven't noticed, when Mom is happy, everyone in the household seems to be happy. Many men do not seem to realize the great asset they have in a happy spouse.

Some men beat their wives down verbally in public with such statements as, "This is my old lady." Such putdown statements contribute to a low self-esteem. You also contribute to a low self-esteem in your wife by releasing your frustrations on her rather than dealing with them in prayer or through the godly counsel of a good friend.

When I am frustrated, the easiest place to release it is on my wife, Sharon. Personally, I never notice how dirty the house is until I'm having some challenges, either in the business or in finances. I ask, "How come this house is so dirty? Why is there so much clutter?"

When frustration hits, we always take it out on the ones we love the most and are closest to us. A visual example of this is your car. No matter how great the vehicle, it goes nowhere without gas. How far the vehicle goes is determined by how much gas is in the tank. To help you determine this, automobile manufacturers put a gas gauge to tell you how much you have in the tank. All of us are tolerant to a certain degree. When our self-esteem is high, our tolerance is high as our automobile example illustrates. Our gas tanks are full so our gauge is on F (full).

As we get frustrated and the pressures of life get to us, our tolerance level drops, going towards E (empty). When

29

we hit E, our vehicle stops or in human terms, we get frustrated with everything — wife, work, business, kids, and yes, even God.

It's extremely important you don't let your gauge get to E. How do we do that? By staying in God's Word! By looking for God's purpose in your life and seeing where you can help others less fortunate.

Both men and women often compare their spouse's underdeveloped talents with someone else's developed talents, thus making themselves feel inferior. It has been said that the root of unhappiness is comparison. If you try to compare your spouse with someone else's spouse, you will always be unhappy. I am more athletic than Sharon, so if I compare her with someone else's wife who is more athletic, I am in trouble, because we then begin to focus on the negatives.

Some couples get in trouble because they look at what they don't have as opposed to what they do have. This breeds discontent.

God created each person unique and special, so if we focus on that uniqueness, there will be no need for comparison. The attitude of competition with others will then be eliminated.

When the husband brings a sensitive issue to his wife's attention, such as weight, if it isn't handled right, it will lower her self-esteem. It takes a tremendous amount of success and guts to build confidence and restore one's self-esteem. Any help you can give your spouse in building her self-esteem will pay great dividends.

One of the saddest things any child can experience is to be a part of unhappy parents. Unhappy people tend to vent their frustrations on those closest to them. Sometimes children become the escape valve for their parent's frustration. Rarely do children understand that they are not the cause of their parent's problem. A healthy self-image in children is threatened because of lack of confidence and self-esteem on the part of parents.

Moms and Dads, let's get it together...together! We can change the world by changing our own families.

Here are some strategic guidelines for husbands in helping their wives become happier and more effective people.

Always look for the good in your wife. Easy? No. Valuable? Yes. If you look for the good in your wife, then change becomes a natural by-product of building her up. It brings encouragement. However, if you say, "I won't approve of you unless you lose weight or unless you do this or that," you are creating an atmosphere for competition and resentment. Then there will be disagreements over the toothpaste and other trivial things, yet the toothpaste isn't the real issue!

Before attempting to change a characteristic in your spouse, ask, "What is the one thing I do that you would like to see me eliminate or change?" Don't make a bargain like, "I'll change this if you'll change that!" You must first desire to change and please your wife. When the changes occur in you, you will motivate your wife to examine herself and want to change because she sees a sincere change in you.

What do you do if you change and correct the faults your wife points out in you, but she doesn't respond? Ask her again, "What is the next thing you would like to see me eliminate or change?" You may have to ask a third, fourth, or fifth time. If your spouse never changes, which I doubt will happen because kindness begets kindness, you will have gained in learning much more about yourself.

Problems exist in a marriage where each partner believes he, or she, can change the other. Accept your mate for who he/she is, and let God do the changing.

Women tend to be more sensitive than men. When your wife sees how hard you are working to please her, she will, most likely, want to change to please you.

When you are looking for the good in your wife, the power of praise will enrich your relationship. You can praise your wife by saying, "Honey, that was a wonderful dinner," or "That dress looks great on you!"

Christ always built people up rather than tear them down. Building your wife up will enhance her self-esteem, which, in turn, will enrich your relationship with her.

Be more sensitive to your wife's needs. Women need to be hugged. They need to be told how much you love them, and occasional flowers are a must! In our house, we take hug breaks. It's tough for some guys to hug, because they were raised in families where no affection was shown.

The best way to raise great children is to let them see a good marriage. What they see modeled in the marriage of their parents is a key in determining their own value.

Your wife needs to know how important she is in your life. Men tend to think that bringing home the paycheck says, "I love you," but women need to be told, "I love you." Most women would rather live in a modest home with love and affection than in a palace with no expression of feelings.

Twenty years ago, Sharon wasn't as strong as she is today and neither was I. She loved flowers, and I thought they were a waste of money. I stopped by a roadside stand and bought her a bouquet of flowers for 50 cents. Now, that was hard for me to spend the 50 cents because I truly thought it was a waste of money. I was kind of proud of myself that I had finally broken down and bought her some.

When I gave her the flowers, she said, "Where did you get these? At a 50 cent roadside stand?" Her words stung, and I allowed the hurt to take residence in my heart. Even though we loved each other, within myself I said, "I will never buy any more flowers for her." So for ten years I didn't! I was nursing my own ego by denying her flowers rather than being sensitive to her needs.

God wired women and men differently. A man makes a mistake to think his wife will automatically like everything he likes.

Paul talks about submission *to each other* as husband and wife. We cannot expect our wives to be submissive to us unless we are submissive to Christ. Let's look at this account in Ephesians 5:21-33:

> *Submit to one another* out of reverence for Christ.
>
> Wives, submit to your husbands as to the Lord.
>
> For the husband is the head of the wife as Christ is the head of the church, his body, of which he is the Savior.
>
> Now as the church submits to Christ, so also wives should submit to their husbands in everything.
>
> Husbands, love your wives, just as Christ loved the church and gave himself up for her
>
> To make her holy, cleansing her by the washing with water through the word,
>
> And to present her to himself as a radiant church, without stain or wrinkle or any other blemish, but holy and blameless.
>
> In this same way, husbands ought to love their wives as their own bodies. He who loves his wife loves himself.
>
> After all, no one ever hated his own body, but he feeds and cares for it, just as Christ does the church —
>
> For we are members of his body.
>
> "For this reason a man will leave his father and mother and be united to his wife, and the two will become one flesh."
>
> This is a profound mystery — but I am talking about Christ and the church.
>
> However, each one of you also must love his wife as he loves himself, and the wife must respect her husband.

Philippians 2:5-11 says Jesus Christ submitted Himself to the Father and *became a servant*, just as we husbands are to be servants to our wives.

Your attitude should be the same as that of Christ Jesus:

Who, being in very nature God, did not consider equality with God something to be grasped,

But made himself nothing, taking the very nature of a servant, being made in human likeness.

And being found in appearance as a man, he humbled himself and became obedient to death — even death on a cross!

Therefore God exalted him to the highest place and gave him the name that is above every name,

That at the name of Jesus every knee should bow, in heaven and on earth and under the earth,

And every tongue confess that Jesus Christ is Lord, to the glory of God the Father.

True submission is cheerful obedience to authority. God appointed the husband to be head of the home just as Jesus Christ is head of the Church (the entire Body of believers).

If the husband requires anything of his wife that is contrary to God's will, she should obey God. No one is called to submit to physical or sexual abuse, violence or continual verbal abuse. Christ never abused anyone. That doesn't mean a wife doesn't accept an angry moment from her husband when he is frustrated, but abuse has no place in any relationship.

God will always bless the man who *serves* his family and models his behavior (his words and actions) after the example of Christ. The husband who serves people and causes others to win is going to prosper.

Make plans together, such as goal-setting for family vacations, the children's college fund and business goals. Including your wife in making plans and goal-setting will increase her sense of importance to you.

Getting it together . . . together with your wife in goal-setting is strategic in identifying the direction in which you need to move to become the persons you want to be. Setting big goals means you will have to develop into a big person to achieve them. You will have to care more, help more and simply do more for others. Jesus said, **For everyone to whom much is given, from him much will be required** (Luke 12:48, NKJV).

Vacations provide a great avenue for family bonding. Equally as important are the special vacations that you and your wife take alone. It helps to keep romance in your relationship. Do something radical with your wife occasionally, like spending a week-end in San Francisco, New Orleans, or somewhere she enjoys.

Growing older with your wife is a tradition that needs to be reinstated in our society. The benefits far exceed the effort to make it happen. Sharon and I are extremely blessed to have both of our parents entering their senior years together. We want to take this opportunity to thank my parents, Frank and Rita Delisle, who celebrated their 50th wedding anniversary and Sharon's parents, Thurman and Virginia Richards, who celebrated their 48th anniversary. Their role model of work, sacrifice, giving and helping each other is something we have watched and enjoyed.

Take control. No woman wants a wimpy husband she can twist around her finger and manipulate all the time. The husband is called to be the spiritual head of the home. **Now I want you to realize that the head of every man is Christ, and the head of the woman is man, and the head of Christ is God** (1 Cor. 11:3).

Most men fall short of what God intends for them to be, particularly in taking the reigns of spiritual leadership and direction in the home. When the spiritual leadership of the home is in order, the husband's other responsibilities will be easier.

The husband needs to take the reigns of financial leadership and be responsible for paying the bills. I believe it puts a tremendous amount of pressure on the wife to handle the family budget. In addition to taking care of the family and trying to keep the husband happy, it is okay for the wife to pay the bills as long as the husband knows what is going on. A husband is less likely to make unnecessary purchases when he knows the state of the family's finances. (Getting it together in your finances is discussed further in Chapter 8.)

Prioritizing your time. If men spent 25 percent of the time that they devote to their careers with their wives, many wives would be happier and the marriage relationship would be strengthened.

Men love to conquer, to be successful and to have prestige and respect in the work place. This is great if...

- Your spiritual and family life are strong.

- Your marriage is consistently growing stronger.

- Your children have a growing relationship with you.

The husband who will see that these things are in place is living to the fullest, and he will bring the same quality of life to his wife and children. Men, can we do it? Yes! Will we do it? It's up to each of us!

Bible Study

INSTRUCTIONS: Be honest with yourself as you complete this study. If you are studying in a group or with your family, share those things you feel most comfortable in sharing. Do one question each day for the next week, or spend thirty minutes completing the entire study at one time.

For Couples...

1. As a spouse, take a moment to think of at least ten things that you appreciate about your partner. Now, sit face to face and have the wife share first the ten things she appreciates about her spouse. Then have the husband share the ten things that he appreciates about his wife.

    - Whenever the opportunity arises, be sure to tell your spouse what you like about him/her.

2. Read together Ephesians 5:21-33. Now share with one another the following:

    - The verse that means the most to me is _____

    - The verses most difficult for me are_____

3. As a couple, fill out the following goals or vision you have for your marriage:

    In a year, we will be_____

    _____

    _____

    In five years, we will be_____

    _____

    _____

    In ten years, we will be_____

    _____

    _____

    (Write down any plans that you believe you have as a couple.Write down your understanding of future plans separately, and then share with one another what you have written down. Look at the similarities and differences.)

4. As a couple, share what are the main differences you see between men and women in marriage.

5. Now, husbands sit quietly while your wife shares for five minutes the ways you can be more effective as a husband and/or father in your family. Do not discuss this, simply listen and receive. Husbands, you will be able to share about your wives in the next Bible study. Do not make any comment, simply receive and then:

   • Wives, have your husbands kneel and place your hands on their shoulders or head and pray God's blessing on them.

6. Read 1 Peter 3:7. According to this scripture, what area is hindered if you do not treat your wife properly?

   _____

7. Read Numbers 20:1-13. What did God ask Moses to do to provide water for the Israelites where there was no water in the natural? (Verse 8)

   _____
   _____
   _____
   _____

   Did Moses obey the direction of the Lord?

   _____ Yes   _____ No

   If not, explain what he did (Verse 11). _____
   _____
   _____

   What was the result of Moses' disobedience (Verse 12)?
   _____
   _____
   _____
   _____

What spiritual principle would you derive from this account for the husband's leadership in the home?

_____

_____

_____

_____

8. According to Ephesians 5:23, the husband is head of the wife as Christ is head of the Church. What are some of the Christlike qualities that should be evident in the husband's leadership?

_____

_____

_____

_____

_____

For Families...

1. As a family, have everyone gather around in a circle and then have the fathers tell the mothers all the things in one minute they appreciate about her in being a wife or mother. Once that is done, have the wife say the same kinds of affirmations for the husband. This is done so that the children can listen to their mothers and fathers affirm one another.

2. Now, invite the children to make a list of all the things that they appreciate about their parents, not as parents but as models of husbands and wives.

3. As a family, read Ephesians 5:21-33. Discuss as a family all the different characteristics husbands and wives are to have in a marriage.

4. Now, invite the children in the family to share what they believe the most important quality of being a husband or being a wife is. Then have the parents share the most important quality. Once this sharing is completed, discuss how your ideas are similar or different.

5. Invite everyone in the family to pray for each other. This might be done as follows:

   - The children can pray for their parents, thanking God for them as model husbands and wives.

   - The parents might pray for their children, thanking God for the gift of their children that God has entrusted to them.

   - The husband might pray for the wife and the wife for the husband in front of the children so that they might see their parents praying for one another.

   - The father and mother might pray out loud for the whole family so that the children can see how they, as a couple, pray for their family.

4

"Get It Together" — Husband

A wife must first recognize that God created her husband unique and special, and because he is unique and special, she should not compare him with other men. Once you begin to compare your husband with other men, nagging and manipulation often result in an attempt to change him. Women, you can't change your husbands, but God can!

Encourage your husband. Many wives do not realize how significant their words of encouragement are to their husbands, nor do they realize how destructive nagging and fault-finding are. Any wife who will make her husband feel like a king and a hero will eventually be made the queen she deserves to be. I use the word *eventually* because women many times want to see change in their husbands faster than they are capable of changing. Most men need a lot of positive reinforcement.

Men tend to be more logical than women. This is one of the reasons why men aren't as sensitive to her needs as they should be at times. The pressure of work, the drive for accomplishment and success and the fear of looking silly or stupid paralyze men from action. Yet, inside they feel much more sensitive, romantic and open than they dare let their spouse know because of fear.

It should be the wife's goal to build her husband's confidence to the point he can break through the walls of fear that have tried to hold him back from becoming the man God has created him to be. She can do this first by letting him know that she believes in him, and second, by availing herself to do whatever she can to be a support to him.

Appreciate your husband. The wife should express her appreciation for the way her husband takes care of the home, the car, the boat, finances, etc. She should praise him for his good points, and pray about the qualities that need to be strengthened. The wife should pray for her husband to have wisdom and discernment to lead the family.

Sometimes wives expect husbands to fulfill their every need, yet Christ is the only One who can fulfill all of their needs.

Honor your husband. To honor your husband is to let him be the leader and make yourself vulnerable to his leadership. To honor him does not mean you approve of everything he does. You may be wondering, "How do you honor a jerk?" There are times when it is difficult to show honor to the husband because of his behavior and lack of headship in the home, but every woman can honor his position just as she would honor her pastor's position or the president's position. The wife is not obligated to submit to or follow anything that is against Biblical principles.

First Timothy 2:1,2 says:

> **I urge, then, first of all, that requests, prayers, intercession and thanksgiving be made for everyone —**
> **For kings and all those in authority** [that includes husbands and daddies], **that we may live peaceful and quiet lives in all godliness and holiness.**

As you praise and honor your husband, it must be done with honesty and integrity. In other words, honor and respect him without hypocrisy. Most husbands will respond to praise and respect that are sincere.

To stand by your husband with encouragement and respect will help to strengthen his confidence and self-esteem. As he surrenders to the lordship of Jesus Christ, his confidence will again be strengthened and his spiritual growth will bring stability to the wife and children.

Build the bond of trust. The wife's relationship with her husband cannot grow beyond the bond of trust that exists between them. Trust is built, and the starting point for building it is to first trust God.

To build trust, the wife must love her husband. She must care enough to converse. Communication, obviously, is a key to a strong marriage. Trust is built when both the wife and the husband are good listeners. To trust is for the wife to say, "You make a decision, honey, and I will follow" (without saying), "I told you so." Trusting him is allowing him to make a mistake. This is where the wife must simply trust God because **we know that in all things God works for the good of those who love him, who have been called according to his purpose** (Rom. 8:28).

God can use mistakes to bring the husband and wife closer together and to strengthen the husband's leadership skills. The husband's growth in ability to lead takes place over a process of time. He will learn from his mistakes as the wife encourages him rather than deflates him with demeaning words and actions.

Love your husband. To trust is for the wife to communicate her commitment to her husband: "Honey, I believe in you for the long haul." Men need to know the wife is committed.

First Corinthians 13:4-8a describes what love is:

> **Love is patient, love is kind. It does not envy, it does not boast, it is not proud.**
>
> **It is not rude, it is not self-seeking, it is not easily angered, it keeps no record of wrongs.**
>
> **Verses 4,5**

If a wife is going to trust her husband, she should not keep a secret notebook recording the number of times he fails!

> **Love does not delight in evil but rejoices with the truth.**
>
> **It always protects, always trusts, always hopes, always perseveres.**
>
> **Love never fails.**
>
> **Verses 6-8a**

Love always believes the best in your spouse. Just because the husband strikes out one time (so did Babe Ruth!!) doesn't mean he shouldn't take a swing again! If he gets bucked off the horse, he should climb back on and take another ride with the wife cheering him on, "I'm for you, honey!"

Make your husband feel like a king! A man's greatest needs are the approval of his wife, respect from his children and success at work. Sharon always made our children, particularly when they were small, realize that Dad was the reason they got new clothes. She always built me up in front of the children when I came home from work and made me feel like their hero! That makes you want to come home!

The husband who gets beat up in the world, then comes home and is never treated with respect, will start spending more time away from home — in the bar, on the golf course, in the bowling alley, or with another woman who will build him up.

Proverbs 21:1 says, **The king's heart is in the hand of the Lord; he directs it like a watercourse wherever he pleases.** If God can turn the heart of a king, He is capable of turning the husband's heart. It is important that the wife trust in the lordship of Christ, because in Him alone is the deep security she needs.

Encourage your husband in decision-making. Sharon used to help me make decisions by making the statement, "Dennis, don't you think it would be a good idea to do such-and-such?" It took several years before I realized that she was really directing my decisions, but she let me think I was making them! There came a time when I became the decision-maker because my walls of fear about making wrong choices were brought down. I included her in the decision-making process, but I took the lead.

There is strength and wisdom in a godly mentor. The role of a mentor for both husbands and wives — when the fruit of the older person is admirable, godly and pure — can be highly beneficial. Titus 2:4-7 confirms the idea of mentorship, with older men teaching younger men and older women teaching younger women.

Then they [the older women] can train the younger women to love their husbands and children,

To be self-controlled and pure, to be busy at home, to be kind, and to be subject to their husbands, so that no one will malign the word of God.

Similarly, encourage the young men to be self-controlled.

In everything set them an example by doing what is good.

The role of a mentor is to help produce fruit in your life similar to that which is being produced in his or her life. I want to take this opportunity to thank Dexter Yager for being a mentor in my life. I sincerely hope you find such a person in your life, too! Jesus said, A tree is recognized by its fruit (Matt. 12:33b).

Wives, determine to be the best wife you can be to your husband. Determine to align yourself with the virtuous woman described in Proverbs 31:10-31 (NKJV):

Who can find a virtuous wife? For her worth is far above rubies.

The heart of her husband safely trusts her; so he will have no lack of gain.

She does him good and not evil all the days of her life.

She seeks wool and flax, and willingly works with her hands.

She is like the merchant ships, she brings her food from afar.

She also rises while it is yet night, and provides food for her household, and a portion for her maidservants.

She considers a field and buys it; from her profits she plants a vineyard.

She girds herself with strength, and strengthens her arms,

She perceives that her merchandise is good, and her lamp does not go out by night.

She stretches out her hands to the distaff, and her hand holds the spindle.

She extends her hand to the poor, yes, she reaches out her hands to the needy.

She is not afraid of snow for her household, for all her household is clothed with scarlet.

She makes tapestry for herself; her clothing is fine linen and purple.

Her husband is known in the gates, when he sits among the elders of the land.

She makes linen garments and sells them, and supplies sashes for the merchants.

Strength and honor are her clothing; she shall rejoice in time to come.

She opens her mouth with wisdom, and on her tongue is the law of kindness.

She watches over the ways of her household, and does not eat the bread of idleness.

Her children rise up and call her blessed; her husband also, and he praises her:

"Many daughters have done well, but you excel them all."

Charm is deceitful and beauty is vain, but a woman who fears the Lord, she shall be praised.

Give her of the fruit of her hands, and let her own works praise her in the gates.

Bible Study

INSTRUCTIONS: Be honest with yourself as you complete this study. If you are studying in a group or with your family, share those things you feel most comfortable in sharing. Do one question each day for the next week, or spend thirty minutes completing the entire study at one time.

For Couples...

1. As a couple, look over the following list, and then respond to the suggestions that are given:

    • Encourage your husband.

    • Appreciate your husband.

    • Honor your husband.

    • Build the bond of trust.

    • Love your husband.

    • Make your husband feel like a king.

    • Encourage your husband in decision-making.

    After you have looked over these suggestions, share with one another the following:

    • Which one does each of you feel the wife does best?

    • Which one does each of you feel the wife needs to grow more in doing?

2. Read together Titus 2:4-7. Share with each other how the wife in your family might practically do the encouragement and mentoring spoken of in this passage.

3. Read Proverbs 31:10-31 out loud. Substitute your wife's name for the words "wife" and "she" in the passage. Wives, sit quietly as your husbands did during the last session and listen while the husbands share ways you might be more effective as a Christian wife or mother in your family.

4. Husbands, ask your wife to kneel down while you place your hands on her head or shoulders. Pray God's blessing on her.

5. Read 1 Corinthians 13:4-8a. Please name fifteen characteristics of love as described in these verses:

a. _____

b. _____

c. _____

d. _____

e. _____

f. _____

g. _____

h. _____

i. _____

j. _____

k. _____

l. _____

m. _____

n. _____

o. _____

For Families...

1. Give everyone in your family a magazine. The best magazine might be something like *Time*, *Newsweek*, or *People*. Ask each person in the family to find a picture in the magazine that most depicts:

   • Something about what an ideal mother should be.

   • Something about what an ideal mother should not be.

   Once everyone has chosen a picture, go around the family and have each person share his/her picture and explain why it was chosen.

2. Read out loud as a family Proverbs 31:10-31. Once it has been read out loud, ask each person in the family, except the wife/mother, to share which quality best describes the wife/mother in the family.

3. After everyone has shared them as a family, write a prayer of thanksgiving for the wife/mother. Then read the prayer out loud for the mother/wife.

5

"Get It Together" — Children

What is the key to success in raising your children? I believe the primary key is to love, love, love and love them some more!

Children are a precious gift from God. Psalm 127:3-5 (NKJV) says:

> **Behold, children are a heritage from the Lord, the fruit of the womb is a reward.**
>
> **Like arrows in the hand of a warrior, so are the children of one's youth.**
>
> **Happy is the man who has his quiver full of them; they shall not be ashamed, but shall speak with their enemies in the gate.**

As with other gifts, through use and familiarity, sometimes we grow so used to them that we forget how special and valuable they really are.

Let's review a few principles for raising your children that I believe will help you.

Become involved with your children. Sharon and I were married five years before we had our daughter, Annette. During this time, we lived very busy lives, with Sharon working as a secretary and I was going to San Jose State University to get my B.S. Degree in Accounting. At that same time, we were building our networking business four or five nights a week. It often involved one or two week-end functions each month. We were living at a fast pace.

Our business was growing so well that the corporation offered us a week on their yacht in the Caribbean. It was a wonderful, inspiring week of building beautiful memories — the greatest being the conception of our first child, Annette.

Some of our business associates at that time said, "Now you can't do this or that because you have a child," but our business grew at an even faster rate. We have always looked at our children as our reason for accomplishing things in life as opposed to using them for our excuse to hide our fears or laziness.

Sharon brought Annette to many of our home meetings. She would breast feed Annette in private, lay her down in a semi-darkened area of the home where we were and then join me in the business presentation. Once we had our second child, Dennis, Jr., we did not take both of them on business presentations. It was too difficult with two children.

Sharon and I loved to travel, and the children didn't curtail this part of our lives. We took them with us to Hawaii, Mexico (which I wouldn't recommend for small children) and all over the United States. We had a few challenges with colds and ear problems on airplanes, but the thrill of having them with us was worth it for the bonding and growth together as a family unit. Moms and Dads still need to travel without the children at times to enhance their relationship.

The greatest calling for a mother is in raising the children, but attention must be given to keep the spouse involved and to keep the marriage relationship healthy. If the wife makes the children the principal purpose of her life, then when they are grown and leave home, the relationship with her spouse often must be rebuilt.

Involvement in your children's activities sometimes means sacrifice. Having a parent at home when the child's school day is over provides an openness to discuss challenges, which enriches the child's growth. Because of the high cost of living in today's society, both parents work in many cases. I believe it is worth being creative so the mother can be home during a child's critical years. (For most children, it is important to be available during the first five years and somewhere around sixth grade when they come home from school.)

Parents should support as many of their children's activities as possible. Support the event by supporting the child. Tell him/her why you think they will do great. You can't always be physically at each event or game but you can support them mentally and verbally. Knowing you care and want them to do their best is a major importance to children.

Parents should not try to relive their lives through their children, routing them into the areas of parental interests. This can cause a mental strain and even resentment in the children. Find out exactly what the child wants to do, then support and encourage growth in these events. If you have a soccer star, don't try to make him a baseball star. Take the time to find out what interests and motivates your children.

It takes discipline as a parent to change hats between having your own business or career and spending time with your children at their activities. Parents sometimes tend to become over-involved in attempting to give their children what they did not have as a child. In such cases, parents are driven by guilt.

There is a healthy balance that can be achieved so you can have a happy family life together. For example, one little boy wanted his daddy to help him learn to play catch. The dad was very busy doing catch-up tasks. Every minute the son would come in the den and say, "Daddy, let's play catch."

Finally, because he was driving his dad nuts, the dad took a map of the world and ripped it into several pieces. Since his son was only six years old, he knew it would be difficult for the boy to put the map together quickly. He told his son he would play catch with him once he got the map together. The dad knew this would give him time to do his work.

The son returned in a matter of minutes with the map taped together. The astonished father asked, "Son, how could you get the map together so soon? You don't know where South America or Europe is." The son replied, "I didn't know about all the countries, but on the back of the map was a picture of a man, so when I put the man together, the map of the world went together, too." The dad dropped his pencil and went out to play ball with his son!

One year Sharon and I were going to be gone on Annette's birthday. While we were gone, the lady who took care of the children gave her a birthday party. In school she had a birthday party. When we got home, we gave her another party. She said, "I hope you leave every time my birthday comes, because I got three parties this year!"

Building faith in your children. It is important for your children to realize that they didn't arrive by accident nor are they a generic goof-up! They are very special, created in God's image and likeness and have a divine purpose in life. Faith in God will develop purpose in your children's lives.

The knowledge that they are special will strengthen their self-worth and self-esteem to the point they will be able to resist the temptations of drugs, sex and misconduct encouraged by their peers.

Faith is first learned in children by the example given by their parents, and second, by being a part of a church support group. As parents mature spiritually, it will be reflected in their children who, in turn, will affect future generations. Parents are the primary teachers of their children's values.

Family devotions are great for strengthening the family unit. As you kneel together and pray, the children will be molded by the submissiveness to God they see in their parents, and they will also begin to realize that they are responsible to God for their actions. Let the children be involved in devotion time by sharing scriptures and then discussing, as a family, how to apply the principles of God's Word to daily living.

> Hear, O Israel: The Lord our God, the Lord is one.
>
> Love the Lord your God with all your heart and with all your soul and with all your strength.
>
> These commandments that I give you today are to be upon your hearts.
>
> Impress them on your children. Talk about them when you sit at home and when you walk along the road, when you lie down and when you get up.
>
> Deuteronomy 6:4-7

Build your children's self-esteem. Looking for the good instead of the bad in your children will help them develop an attitude of, "I'm okay." It takes ten positive statements to counteract one negative statement.

Correcting a child's mistakes should not be used as an opportunity to scold or belittle them. Mistakes can be the springboard for greater spiritual growth and understanding. Learn to separate the child from his or her actions.

Don't compare your children with other children. For example, "I wish you were like Susie. She gets A's on her report card." This is one of the quickest ways to destroy your child's self-esteem because it's a putdown. Genuine love isn't based on performance.

Ground rules should be established for your children. Let them know how far they can go. If they make a decision to go beyond your boundaries, then they will have to pay for the consequences of their decisions. Don't set rules that you know you are not going to keep or correct. Take a tough stand on the major rules rather than on the minor ones.

In our home, a "B" average means you can drive the car and have a social life. Anything below a B means you aren't putting proper effort into your school work and therefore some of your privileges are curtailed until the grades improve. If your child needs extra help, it's up to you to help them or hire a tutor.

Children

Children need goals to make their lives rewarding and efficient. A person who has goals will schedule his or her time and events to accomplish them. Our daughter Annette is a great example of goal-setting. When she was eight years old and part of a Brownie Troop, she set a goal to sell 100 boxes of Girl Scout cookies. By selling 100 boxes, she would earn a super cookie patch for her uniform. She placed her goal on our refrigerator where it could be seen and started making phone calls to sell cookies. Call by call, she worked toward her goal.

Sharon overheard Annette explain what a "goal" is to her friends. She said, "First, you write the number on a sheet of paper. Then you tape it to the refrigerator so you can see it each day. Then you make your calls."

As adults, we sometimes fail to grasp the importance of goal-setting. This is why some people's lives are controlled by circumstances rather than by a proper reaction to goals. Why not post your goals on the refrigerator so your children can see your goals? Your example of working, planning and achieving will encourage them.

Another tip I learned from Annette is that she sent thank you cards to everyone who helped her reach her goal. The success of the super cookie patch inspired her to earn a new bike from school candy sales. This required her to sell a tremendous amount of candy, but she set her goal, put it up on the refrigerator and started making her calls.

As she made her calls, she told her customers that her goal was a new bike and expressed appreciation for their help. Once she achieved her goal and received the new bike, we took a picture of her on the bike and sent copies, signed by Annette on the back, to the individuals who helped her reach her goal. The extra effort on Annette's part made the difference between success and super success. Through these experiences, Annette's self-esteem was boosted to a new level.

Bond with your children. We have taken many family trips, some of which were wonderful and others tough. Some of what I call the "toughest" trips were the most conducive to family bonding.

A recent "bonding experience" was a trip to a family reunion in a resort area where the rooms were $29 for four people per night. (My wife's idea of camping and roughing it is bad room service at a Hyatt Regency.) The resort area provided a wonderful memory for our entire family. The week-end made us appreciate what we had at home!

Because it was such a different experience, we coined the expression, "We're bonding" with our children. Now, any time a situation becomes uncomfortable, we say, "We are bonding."

It is important to have your children taught by someone with the same value structure. This reinforcement in your school, church and friends helps your child's confidence that they are doing right. The more reinforcement, the less they'll listen to the wrong peer group.

Make your home a sanctuary for your children. Because of the fast pace of our society today, it is easy for children to feel unloved and unwanted. Never make your children feel like they are a burden. Remember, they are gifts from God.

When our children were younger, Sharon and I hosted many of their activities so we could control the environment. Usually, we had them bring their friends to our house rather than our children going to other homes.

The mother of one of Annette's friends was a single mom who was living with a man to whom she was not married. Annette wanted to spend the night with this friend. When we wouldn't allow it, Annette said, "I don't understand." We explained that her friend could come to our home, but we said, "We cannot allow you to spend the night in a home where they are going against God's principles."

Make every effort to keep communication channels open with your children. Sharon is a wonderful listener and rarely lets any discussion shock her. Some of the things that are talked about and are seemingly "normal" to other children are just plain shocking to us. Sharon listens, absorbs what is happening and then asks, "Well, how do you feel about that?"

Another reason for a strong spiritual life is you can ask your children, "What does God feel about this or that?" We go to the scriptures and seek God's advice.

We want our children to feel comfortable at home. We want them to feel comfortable to invite friends over because we can control the environment at our house. Their friends love coming to our house, because we have fun. Sometimes we take them to a movie with us and go out and have a sandwich together. We always make room for laughter!

Purposefully, we have kept our children in a protective environment because we don't want to throw them to the wolves at a young age. Once they are established in Biblical principles, they will have ample opportunity to combat the principles of the world.

One area of our children's growth we kept an eye on was their response to peers. When Dennis, Jr. was little, there was a boy who wanted to play with him often. This child did not have the discipline and role models in his life that our son had in his. The boy was allowed much more freedom. We knew that Dennis could be a good influence on this boy so we allowed them to play together. Sharon watched carefully to see that Dennis was influencing the boy and not the other way around. If he had influenced Dennis negatively, then Dennis would not have been allowed to play with him anymore.

Releasing your children. One of the major challenges we faced with our children was being O.P. — over-protective. We knew they were special gifts from God, so we took our roles seriously to be proper caretakers.

Releasing and letting go of your children when they leave home is never easy. When Annette left for college, Sharon cried every day for months.

I believe it is easier to let go of your children if you give them progressive freedom where they can learn to be responsible and be given more freedom as they make the right choices.

Not only should you expect your children to respect and obey the guidelines you establish for them, but parents need to show them some of the same courtesies. When Sharon and I were traveling, we would call and let our children know that we were safe and sound.

Letting go of your children doesn't mean cutting them off. You will always be parents, so keep your hearts open to them.

A common phrase of many parents after raising their children is, "If only I had known." No parent does everything right 100 percent of the time. Sharon and I have told our children, "When you are parents, you can raise your children exactly the way you want. But for now, God has entrusted the parenting job to us, and we are prayerfully trying to do our best. You do not have to agree, but you do have to obey."

As we watch our children grow and as we grow in the process of their growth, there are different stages we can see. Each of these stages is unique and different with each child. You should never expect each child to fit into their brother or sister's model. A mistake many parents make is to compare one child with another. They say things like, "Why can't you be more like Susie? She gets such great grades, etc." You have to work with the strengths of each child and help him/her develop and improve their weaknesses.

I am going to lay out a growth pattern as only an eye mark for you to watch for and grow into. I feel that if you know they are coming, you try to adjust to make the transition easier for you and your child.

Dependent - Every child arrives naked, confused and crying. A child is totally dependent upon its parents for their existence. You will make all the decisions for their growth and safety.

Investigation Time - Early adolescence. They start walking, start mixing with other children, start realizing that some actions and items are okay and others are "no no's."

Directive Time - Mixed in with the investigating time. It's a parent's job to discipline, instruct, punish and reward. You need to teach your child good things happen with proper action and bad things happen — pain happens when they disagree with Mom or Dad (authority figures). Respect for authority will help keep your child in line for the future. You can't let children go wild in their early childhood and expect them to be disciplined in later childhood and adulthood. Discipline is taught and rewarded. Then it is remembered.

Negotiation Time - The time your child realizes he or she can do things with or without Mom and Dad knowing. They also start "feeling their oats." You see a change in actions and responses to your actions or requests. This is a challenging time because you want them to do the right thing through their own reasoning. However, if they don't figure it out on their own, you will have the power to correct their actions to make it right.

(Side Note: Some parents say, "How do I know it's right or what's right?" Go to your reference manual — the Bible. God has given you the blueprint, the rule book, the instruction manual for all your responsibilities and relationships. The more the actions you agree with the Bible, the better the life. The opposite is very true, too!)

This action may mean no dance on Saturday night, no car for a week, no television for a week.

You know what motivates your children. The loss of that helps correct attitudes quickly. At this stage, you as parents do not know all that your child does outside your control. For example, you can tell him/her to drive slowly, but you cannot be in the car each time to see that he/she does. So part of your parenting job is to explain the consequences for actions. By this age they should realize that they are accountable for what they do. Even though you've said it since the Investigation Time stage, sometimes it takes until adulthood to get it.

Cutting Loose Time - This is probably the most difficult time of all. Each child matures at different ages. Knowing when to let go and when to hold on is extremely frustrating. I would recommend a series of tests. For example, be home at 12:00 midnight. As they accomplish that, you can let loose more. The right choices give more freedom. The wrong choices cause more discipline. Also, take time to think about the situation.

Sharon is much better at responding to actions than I am. I tend to react to actions. It's better to get all the facts and understand them before you take corrective actions. (Side Note: Mom and Dad, don't be too big or too adult to say you're sorry when you make a mistake. Remember, you are human, too, and you will make mistakes. Don't make two mistakes by not correcting the first!)

This stage can be identified clearly when a child goes off to college, gets married, or rents their own apartment. They are out, but they are not yet independent totally. They'll still need reinforcement, guidance and a knowing that home is still home.

Independent Time - What time your child reaches this level is sometimes hard to discern. When did you realize you were a grownup? Who knows? Seriously, you know that you know that it's now up to you. You are the adult and your children are adults and you need to treat them as such. Before this time you have been guiding, giving advice, helping them to discern many kinds of information. Now, it's time to cut the strings and see if they can fly. This means no giving advice without being asked. This is a toughy, but many times we must allow our children to make mistakes so that God can use them to teach them. I feel that this is the point when your role changes from parent first to friendship first and then parenting second. Through the other stages, you had to be a parent first and a friend second. Many parents try to be a friend first too soon in a child's development. You were entrusted with this life to mold, direct, nourish and let go. Don't let go of the responsibility too soon, but when the time is right, continue to encourage your child with belief in them but wait until they ask for advice.

I hope that this growth capsule concept has helped you in identifying the bench marks of your child's growth. A blessing for any child is parents who are willing to learn and willing to grow with the growth of their children. Take up the challenge — it's a wonderful experience.

Parents who are blessed with grandchildren have a second shot to take all they have learned and help the grandchildren without offending their own children. You can expose them to the treasures of wisdom you have gained over the years.

As a mother, one of the greatest gifts you can give your children is to love their father. As a father, one of the greatest gifts you can give your children is to love their mother. But the greatest gift of all that a parent can give his or her children is the demonstration of a life fully yielded to God.

Bible Study

INSTRUCTIONS: Be honest with yourself as you complete this study. If you are studying in a group or with your family, share those things you feel most comfortable in sharing. Do one question each day for the next week, or spend thirty minutes completing the entire study at one time.

For Couples...

1. On a piece of paper or a 3x5 card, write down as a father or mother the three most important principles or rules that you have as being a good Christian parent. Once each of you has written down the three rules or principles, share them with one another and then put them in the rank order of their priority. List them below:

   a. _____

   b. _____

   c. _____

   d. _____

   e. _____

   f. _____

2. Now, as a mother and father, each of you take a piece of paper or some stationery and write a letter of appreciation and affirmation to each of your children. Include in that letter a prayer asking for God's blessing and building up of faith in each child. Once those letters have been written, seal them in an envelope and label each envelope with the appropriate name of each child. Give these letters to your children at the next meal you share together as a family.

3. Read together Psalm 127:3-5 as parents. Read it out loud and in unison. Once you have read the Psalm, pray together giving God thanks for your children and ask-

ing for wisdom and guidance in rearing them in the fear
and admonition of the Lord.

4. As a husband, what are some of the ways you demonstrate your love for your wife in the presence of your
   children?

   _____

   _____

   _____

   _____

   _____

5. As a wife, what are some of the ways you demonstrate
   your love for your husband in the presence of your
   children?

   _____

   _____

   _____

   _____

   _____

6. What are some of the ways you make each of your children feel unique, special and valuable?

   _____

   _____

   _____

   _____

   _____

For Families...

1. Give everyone in the family a 3x5 card or a piece of paper on which they can write the name of each person in the family. Now give the instructions that under each person's name, everyone in the family is to write at least five things they appreciate about that person.

   - Once everyone has completed their list, start with the oldest person in the family and share your list with everyone else. Go around the circle until everyone has had the opportunity to share.

2. In the space provided below, each person in the family, without discussing this with anyone else, is to write down what you believe the most important rule or principle is that your family lives by:

   _____

   _____

   _____

   _____

   - Once everyone has written down their most important rule or principle, go around the family and share. After each one has shared as a family, make the list and prioritize in order of importance those principles or rules.

      a. _____

      b. _____

      c. _____

      d. _____

      e. _____

      f. _____

      g. _____

      h. _____

      i. _____

      j. _____

3. Together as a family, read out loud and in unison 1 Corinthians 13. Once everyone in the family has read that out loud and in unison, complete the following sentences:

   • In our family, the quality of love most seen is_____
   _____

   • In our family, the quality that needs to grow the most is _____

4. As a family, form a circle and hold hands. Ask each person in the circle to say a short sentence prayer, giving thanks to God for your family.

For Parents . . .

"Philosophy of Discipline"

1. We are committed to being God's "hands and feet" with our children and recognize that they are on loan to us from God. We will endeavor to keep all of our discipline in line with His Word and His will for our children.

2. We will pray over our children on a regular basis, knowing that not only do they need God's help, but we parents need to have our perception toward them constantly controlled and balanced by the Lord.

3. We commit ourselves to loving each other with a strong, consistent love, knowing that this will ultimately be a great encouragement and tonic for our children's behavior and growth.

4. We are committed to disciplining our children as a team. Whatever situation comes up, neither of us will violate the authority of the other spouse. We will always support one another in front of our children, and if we have any differences about how to discipline them, we will attempt to solve them in private.

5. As a father, I will make a special effort to avoid provoking my children to wrath through the display of a harsh spirit. If my wife points out that I have been harsh toward my children, I will stop and pray about the problem and endeavor, through God's power, to be open to her counsel and willing to correct the problem with my teenagers.

6. As a mother, I will work on being firm with my children. Although I want to be loving at all times, I will strive not to let any merciful feelings I have towards my kids influence me to take their side against my husband. I will endeavor, by God's power, never to step between them and my husband in an attempt to protect them.

7. We will seek, not to punish behavior, but to discipline character. We will endeavor to determine what charac-

ter qualities need to be improved and work at putting together disciplinary action that is appropriate to each need. Our goal will be to help our teenagers see life from God's large frame of reference, and we will therefore endeavor not to let ourselves get bogged down by attempting to press the kids into our own mold.

8. We will work at being patient with our teenagers, avoiding rash statements and actions. We commit ourselves to first understanding our kids and how they feel before attempting to communicate what is on our mind.

9. We will focus on helping our children set and follow after their own long-range goals instead of looking for short-term fixes. We will help them plan ahead for their future, then work together with them to achieve their goals. We understand that we are ultimately working toward our teenagers' independence.[1]

---

[1]Souter, John, *The Teenage Zone*, Tyndale House Publishers, Inc., Wheaton, Illinois, 1994.

6

"Get It Together" — Relationships

By Randal Ross

A well-dressed businessman came into my office. After a short, polite conversation, he blurted out what really brought him there. "Pastor, I'm resigning my membership in the church," he said. I was taken back. "Why, Fred? Has someone offended you? Do you disagree with the teaching of the church?" "No, Pastor," he responded. "I just feel like such a failure. I'm tired of failing. I don't think I'm cut out for this Christianity thing." Then he told me his story, and my heart went out to him.

His second marriage was not working very well. His daughter refused to talk to him, and he was having a hard time getting along with his boss. He just felt like a failure. I put my arm around him and said, "Fred, everyone feels like a failure and wants to quit at times, but you can make it. You're on the right track." And he did make it. His marriage started to improve. His daughter found a wonderful young man who wanted to marry her and asked Dad for advice. Things were even getting better at work.

I'm telling you this story because if you have made it this far in the book, you might feel a little overwhelmed. You might imagine most Christians are totally different than you. You may think that everything is always great for Christians, and that you can't measure up because you have failed in your relationships or dreams.

The truth is, every person has failed in some way. There are no perfect people. Everyone brings dreams, gifts, talents

71

and desires into this life, but as we grow, we also bring our hangups, emotional garbage from the past, unrealistic expectations and plain old blunders. When you put two or more imperfect people together, you are going to experience some emotional fireworks, hurt feelings, misunderstandings, and occasionally, even a few failures.

The Bible tells us that all of us have failed at life. God knows that we are not perfect. This is why He came to help us. One thing I really love about the Bible is that it is so honest with the failures and mistakes of its heroes.

One day Moses got so frustrated and angry with his people that he asked God to kill him. I can't remember asking God to kill me, but I have thought about how much easier it would be if a few people weren't around! Abraham lied about his wife twice. David had an adulterous affair with Bathsheba and killed her husband to cover up her pregnancy. David's family was often a mess, yet God calls him a man after His own heart (Acts 13:22).

Simon Peter, the rock of the Church, wavered over fellowship with ordinary people and was rebuked publicly by Paul. Paul had a fight with his close friend Barnabas and called John Mark a loser, only to realize his mistake years later. I'm not telling you these stories to excuse your failures in relationships and in all of life. The truth is, life and relationships are a challenge, and we are going to fail a few times. But there is good news! *There is a way to avoid many of our failures and to recover when we make a mistake.*

The key to avoiding unnecessary failures and to recover from those that we regret is to *learn to turn our mistakes into growing opportunities.*

The first key to turning your mistakes and failures into opportunities is to be realistic. Being realistic means to have a balanced view of life, including your relationships. Conflict is normal, and as long as you understand that and use it properly, you can use it to achieve even better relationships.

There are two ways to look at conflict. The first is to see conflict as something terrible and unnatural. You may view your conflicts as failure. The second is to see conflict as a symptom, telling you something you need to know about yourself and others. Some people panic when they get into a disagreement or a conflict. They make the mistake of always trying to cover up and stop it. Sometimes it is good to just stop, but many times it is better to find out: What is the conflict or tension telling you?

If you use the conflict to understand the other person, to see their value and show your flexibility, you can improve your relationship with this person. Anyone whose marriage lasts more than two weeks has learned this! Isn't it wonderful to make up after a disagreement? There is often a new awakening of love, value and support. Using disagreement to grow means that your relationship is real rather than phony. You're not living on egg shells but on a foundation of trust, love and commitment.

It is also important to build your tolerance for conflict. This means that you give some room for others to have a bad day. My daughter Jessica is entering into those emotional roller-coaster years of adolescence. Some days there is nothing that is right and everything seems critically wrong. On those days she reminds me of the story of Limburger cheese.

There was a grandfather who fell asleep while reading to his granddaughter. She did not appreciate it so she went to the refrigerator and found some Limburger cheese and rubbed it into his thick mustache as he slept. If you have ever smelled Limburger cheese, you know it stinks! When grandfather woke up, he sniffed the air and said, "My, this room smells." He went into the kitchen and announced, "This kitchen stinks, too." After grandmother told him to get out if he didn't like it, he walked outside and took a long sniff and said, "My Lord, the whole world stinks!"

That's the way it is in life. Some days we wake up with a bad smell in our mind. Nothing anyone does is going to help. We need to build in some allowance for bad days, mistakes and failures. The Bible tells us not to keep account of wrongdoing of others but to let them go and let forgiveness flow.

The longer I am married, the more I understand that something I used to think was important and worth a fight really doesn't matter. I say to myself, "Do I really want to spend the night on the couch? Is it worth it?" Most of the time it's not worth the fight.

Remember, conflict is a part of life. It is part of being different and thinking different. Don't use it to hurt yourself or others, but learn from others so you can be a better person.

The second key to turn your mistakes and failures into opportunities is, decide to learn from your mistakes. Mistakes and failures are hard enough to endure the first time they happen, so don't make the mistake of not learning from them.

It is a natural, human tendency to avoid pain or cover it up with drugs or in some other way, but that is not always wise. Pain is a part of life, and we can learn from it. Pain tells us that something is wrong or something needs to be fixed. When you make a relationship mistake, you need to stop for a minute and ask yourself, *"What really happened?"* With honest effort, you can often find the cause or the trouble spot. Sometimes, however, you can't see why something happened. Then it is time to ask the other person what you did wrong. It is amazing how often we miss this obvious truth. We wonder all night long (sometimes many nights long!) about what happened. We might even ask our friends at work what they think happened or pay a professional to help us figure it out when all we really needed to do was to ask the other person.

When Andrea and I were first married, we had a horrible fight. Really, it wasn't much of a fight. I was wiped out by the atomic bomb of a slammed door in my face and the threat of leaving me. I really didn't know what happened or why she reacted that way. All I said was that I was going to smack her. When I said that, she burst into tears and slammed the door shut. Before you judge me, I really didn't mean I was going to hit her. This was simply a way my family communicated.

My father and mother were very loving and verbal. They came from big families, and you would often hear something like, "If you do that again, I'm going to smack you or beat you within an inch of your life."

Now, no one ever hit us on the head or abused us. No one ever beat us within an inch of our lives. It is hard to explain but what we heard was, "I love you too much to let you go on doing that." We were family, and we were committed at all costs to work things out.

What I was trying to tell my wife was that no matter what, we were a family and we were going to work it out. The problem was, that was not how Andrea heard it. When her father said he was going to hit her, he meant it. He was an alcoholic and would "lose it" at times. He did hit, and hard! I asked Andrea what was wrong and she told me. I learned that day to express that I was committed to her and to love her in a healthier way. I never said it again, but I might never have learned if I had not asked.

You can turn a lot of things around and learn if you honestly ask and listen. Remember to apologize. Many people think apology means they are admitting wrong and the other person is right! It means you are sorry and you want to work things out. The mistake many parents and spouses make is they think if they apologize they will no longer get the respect they deserve and need. The truth is, an apology does not lower you in the eyes of the other person, but it makes you a real hero!

One Sunday morning a staff member brought his children to church with him during staff prayer time. Since it was early, the children were tired and bored. They ended up in a real fight outside the doors of the chapel. I rushed out and told them to be quiet and that they didn't belong there. They were disturbing my prayer time. What I did was right, but how I did it was very wrong. I overreacted and I was loud. I was far too angry, and the punishment was too harsh for the offense.

That night I asked their father to join me and I went to his son, Andrew. When he saw me coming, he flinched and looked for a place to hide. I caught him and put this frightened five year old in front of me. Then I kneeled down on one knee and said, "Andrew, I want you to know that I was wrong this morning. I overreacted and I yelled and that wasn't right. You're not in trouble. It's okay. Will you forgive me?" While his daddy watched, Andrew took my hand and shook it real hard and said, "That's okay, Pastor Ross. I make mistakes, too. You're really a good pastor, and I just think you were tired." He was right.

The next day I received a letter from David, his father. He thanked me for being a man of God enough to admit my mistakes and said he respected me more than ever. I have found those who love us will follow us to the ends of the earth if we are honest and admit our mistakes.

The third key to turning mistakes and failures into opportunities is to let your relationships grow. Many times a struggling relationship is a sign that the relationship needs some air or room to grow. The fact is, no one is stagnant, but we are changing and growing. A healthy relationship needs room to grow. When you don't give each other space and growing room, it starts to hurt just like when you wear shoes that are too small.

This means the person you married may not be the same person he or she was ten years ago. You were both young, and maybe you did some things for her because she wanted them and needed them. But she is ten years older now and she may want to grow in life, experience and learn just as you have been growing at work. If you are wise, you will give her room to fly.

The same lack of growing room can cause unnecessary problems with children. When they are born, they are totally dependent upon us, but as they grow up, they need some space. They need responsibility and trust. The danger is in always seeing them as our babies. Instead, we need to see them as growing young adults.

The classic example is Steve Martin in the wonderful movie, "The Father of the Bride." Remember the terrible time he had letting his family grow up? My daughter, Jessica, made me sit and watch that movie on New Year's Eve. Everyone had a good laugh at my expense. I protested, "But Jessica, you're only ten!" She said, "But I'm getting you ready, Dad." With that, she gave me a kiss, looked me right in the eye and gave me a warning. "If you embarrass me like Steve Martin did his daughter, I would never talk to you again." The point is, every relationship changes. Marriage partners, children, friendships, co-workers and each of us need to be given room to grow.

It is possible to strangle a relationship to death. Sometimes we hold on so tightly that we drive away the very ones we love. My son, Matthew, used to strike terror in the household pets when he was young. When he picked up the cats or puppies, he would love them so hard that he nearly squeezed the air right out of them. We had to tell him, "Matthew, hold those you love a little looser. They have to breathe." He would protest, "But Daddy, I love them so much. I want to squeeze them." I said, "It's okay to love with all your heart, but you have to hold them a little softer because they need to breathe." Matthew finally learned it the hard way. Chance, our older English bulldog, bit him real hard. Matthew never again tried to hold on too tight.

There are times in our relationships when we have to let go, even though it is hard. It is hard for me. I never want to admit defeat. I believe that I can win in any battle, and I have a hard time admitting defeat in a relationship. But the truth is, you won't win in every relationship. Relationships can fail. Sometimes it is because of something we did wrong.

Sometimes it has nothing to do with us at all, but it is something going on inside of the other person.

You have to know when to let others go. Letting go can be very painful. It is a fact of life that not everyone is going to accept your sales pitch, not everyone will want to go out with you and not everyone will want to be your friend. Sometimes you have to let other people out of the cage and let go. Letting go does not mean cutting them off or not caring or loving them. It just means that we understand that relationships involve people, you and another. Everyone has to have the right to choose and that includes you. The good news is, when you give others the freedom to leave, they often come back and the relationship is better than ever.

I have seen hundreds of marriages that looked hopeless, be restored and find new love and greater commitment. I have seen many children who pushed their parents away, return home and have a great family relationship. There is always hope. Remember the prodigal son story of the boy who pushed his father away only to come home to a great party? Miracles will happen in many relationships, but learn to let go. If you find it too hard to let go, seek out someone who can help you with your pain and fears. God understands and there are many books, counselors and mentors who can help you see daylight again.

One final point in getting it together again in your relationships after mistakes and failures is: Learn to turn your back on your failures.

I tell my people that they must never make an idol of their past or their failures. Far too many people make an altar of their pains and failures and spend the rest of their life worshipping at their feet. It is a mistake to think that God wants us to let our past mistakes and failures stop us from moving forward. There is forgiveness in Christ. That means Jesus has taken care of your failures and wants you to move forward with His plan for your life. It's all right to grieve and feel bad when we make mistakes, but we must guard against the tendency to stop dreaming and stop try-ing because we failed once or a hundred times.

The truth is, the best days of your life can follow your worst failures. My dear grandmother once told me, "Son, when you fall down, be sure to fall forward." That means to learn from your mistakes and let them make you a better person. Remember, there was only one perfect Person, Jesus Christ, and He came to pay for our failures and to give us abundant life. It's time to get up and start moving forward with God's plan for your life. Go ahead, dare to leave your failures behind and look to the future and the life God has planned for you. Dare to make the most of it!

Bible Study

INSTRUCTIONS: Be honest with yourself as you complete this study. If you are studying in a group or with your family, share those things you feel most comfortable in sharing. Do one question each day for the next week, or spend thirty minutes completing the entire study at one time.

For Couples...

1. Below are a number of feelings that people at times have when they make mistakes or fail at something. Check as many of these feelings that you have when you make a mistake. Check as many as apply:

   _____ Get depressed

   _____ Feel guilty

   _____ Blame myself

   _____ Blame others

   _____ Deny the failure or mistake

   _____ Feel regret

   _____ Face it immediately and confess it

   _____ Try to avoid, as long as possible, dealing with the mistake

   Once each of you has checked off your feelings, show what you have checked with your spouse and see if they noticed any feeling in you that you didn't notice yourself and share if there are any feelings that they see in you that you did not notice.

2. Share responses to the following statements:

   • I believe the best way to face failure is _____

   • I believe the worst way to face failure is _____

   • The most important resource that God has given us to face failure is _____

3. Think back to a time in your life when you had a significant failure and how much you learned from that failure. With your spouse share:

   • One of the biggest failures I ever had in my life was

   _____

   • What I learned from that failure was _____

   _____

4. Share with each other the one failure from your past that you have the most difficulty in letting go of and why. After this confession, pray with each other that God will give you the power, the grace and the determination to let go.

5. Read together Philippians 4:8. This is a checklist of attitudes we can have toward ourselves and others that can prevent negative attitudes toward the failures of ourselves and others. Look over the following checklist and on a scale of 1 to 5, rank yourself on how well these attitudes are rooted in your thought life with 1 representing *not at all* and 5 representing *all of the time.*

   _____   True

   _____   Honest

   _____   Right

   _____   Pure

   _____   Lovely

   _____   Admirable

   _____   Excellent

   _____   Virtuous

   _____   Praiseworthy

   Share your ranking with your spouse, and then pray for one another that God will work in your thought life and attitudes to help you grow in those areas that need the most maturing.

6. Read Romans 3:23. How many people fail and fall short of God's glory?

_____

Please check one or more of the following feelings you experience most often when you fail:

_____   Anger

_____   Regret

_____   Inferiority

_____   Hurt

_____   Pain

_____   Relief

_____   Other (Specify: _____)

Describe your attitude toward your own failures: _____

_____

_____

What is your attitude toward the failures of others?

_____

_____

_____

7. Read Luke 15:11-32. What does this story of the prodigal son tell you about God's love?

_____

_____

_____

What does it tell you about how others might respond to your failures?

_____

_____

_____

Why did the father allow the prodigal son to leave? ___

_____

_____

_____

Could you let someone go whom you are holding too closely or too tightly?

_____

_____

Is there anyone right now whom you need to let go and release to God?

_____

_____

_____

8. Read Romans 8:1 and 1 John 3:20. What is hard for you to forgive in yourself?

_____

_____

_____

_____

When will you ask for God's forgiveness? _____

_____

When will you forgive yourself? _____

_____

For Families...

1. Ask everyone in the family to think back to a time when they made a great big mistake and everyone in the family found out about it. Ask each person to share what happened and what they learned from that mistake in the family.

2. As a family, go around the table and discuss and share the following:

   - The thing that makes it hard in our family to admit our mistakes is _____
   _____

   - The thing that makes it easy to admit our mistakes in our family is _____
   _____

   - What's hard about forgiving one another in our family is _____
   _____

   - What's easy about forgiving one another in our family is _____
   _____

3. There is a saying that goes, **"There is nothing that you can do that will make me stop loving you."**

   Ask everyone in the family to share their own paraphrase of this statement.

4. Have everyone in the family read silently Romans 3:23. Then read silently Romans 15:1-7. Close your family time together. Find a way to say to each one in the family, "I love you" in various ways. That might be done with a kiss, a hug, a handshake, a shoulder rub, or a creative way to express your acceptance and forgiveness of each one in the family.

7

"Get It Together" — Thinking

What you train yourself to think about will either increase or decrease your chances for success. Proverbs 23:7a (NKJV) says, **For as he thinks in his heart, so is he.**

God created each person unique and special. No other creature on earth is exactly like you. God has equipped you with the capabilities to accomplish whatever you can conceive and believe. To *conceive* is to form a picture in your mind of how to accomplish the task you set out to do. I am not talking about some transcendental meditator proclaiming, "How great I art syndrome." I am talking about using your God-given talents and abilities to accomplish goals and reach your destiny in life, giving the credit to God.

Getting a good mental picture of the man or woman you want to be will help you get it together in your thoughts. See yourself doing the things God has called you to do as they should be done — with excellence!

No one will ever be perfect, but we are to strive for perfection in our spiritual growth, as the writer of Hebrews said, which will positively affect your natural performance. **Therefore, leaving the discussion of the elementary principles of Christ, let us go on to perfection** (Heb. 6:1, NKJV).

First John 3:2 says, **When he [Jesus Christ] appears, *we shall be like him*.** In the growth process to become more like Jesus, we need to keep our thoughts, words and actions positive. If we goof, we can say to ourselves, "That's not like me. I'll do it better next time." When we do great, just like the mental picture of yourself, your self talk should be, "That's just like me!"

Paul gave us a guideline for what we are to think on in Philippians 4:8: **Finally, brothers, whatever is true, whatever is noble, whatever is right, whatever is pure, whatever is lovely, whatever is admirable — if anything is excellent or praiseworthy — think about such things.**

It takes work, discipline and motivation to grow. Your dream (or goal) must be established to keep your motivation strong.

A loser will say, "I can't change. This is just the way I am." You can change! Second Corinthians 10:5 says **we take captive every thought to make it obedient to Christ.** To take thoughts captive and make them obedient to Christ means that we are to align our thoughts with God's Word. Any thoughts that are not in agreement with His Word need to be cast down. It's a decision to break out of a man-made mold into God's mold created just for *you!*

You can make great things happen when you have the attitude, "God will make a way for me to excel in what He has called me to do."

Too many times, when we face obstacles of seeming impossibility, we let them change or destroy our goals. Our thoughts should be, "There is a way to move the obstacle of impossibility out of my way, for scripture says, **The people who know their God shall be strong, and carry out great exploits** (Dan. 11:32b, NKJV).

Always look for the good in every circumstance. Emerson said, "Nothing is good or bad that the mind doesn't make it so." Abraham Lincoln said, "I guess people are about as happy as they make up their minds to be." You can always find something good in all adversity if you look for it.

To change is to grow and with growth comes pain. You can live with the pain of growth or live with the pain of regret that you didn't move forward in spite of circum-stances. To accept the pain of growth will cause you to see dreams fulfilled and to envision exciting new opportunities.

As far as the pain of regret is concerned, you will find people blaming others for their lack of success, insecurity, resentment and negative thoughts, words and actions. Achievers won't want to be around this kind of person.

Growth is the process of changing to become a better person, which will affect the people around you as well as improve your image of yourself. When you like yourself, you will like other people better, as well.

As you grow in your thoughts, words and actions to be a better person, you become part of the process of changing our world. What better way to change the world than by having God-fearing, God-abiding leaders.

Bible Study

INSTRUCTIONS: Be honest with yourself as you complete this study. If you are studying in a group or with your family, share those things you feel most comfortable in sharing. Do one question each day for the next week, or spend thirty minutes completing the entire study at one time.

For Couples...

1. As a couple, share what you think it means to be:
   - A winner
   - A loser
   - A positive person
   - A negative person
   - Created in the image of God
   - Becoming like Jesus

2. Read the following scriptures out loud as a couple:
   - Proverbs 23:7a
   - 1 John 3:2
   - 2 Corinthians 10:2-6

   The Bible encourages us to think with the mind of Christ and to dwell on those things that are pleasing to God. What thought do you have for one another as a spouse which would please God? Spend one minute each telling one another the thoughts that you have for each other which are positive and pleasing to God.

3. From the list below of Biblical names for believers, choose two that most fit your partner. Share which ones you have chosen with your partner and why.
   - Warrior
   - Saint
   - Sheep

- Prayer intercessor
- Royalty
- Child of God
- Disciple
- Believer
- Priest
- Friend of God
- Man/Woman of God

For Families...

1. The Bible has names for believers. Below is a list of names. Choose one that fits each person in your family. Tell them which one you have chosen and why.

   • Warrior

   • Saint

   • Sheep

   • Prayer intercessor

   • Royalty

   • Child of God

   • Disciple

   • Believer

   • Priest

   • Friend of God

   • Man/Woman of God

2. Go around the circle of your family and complete the following sentence for each person in your family.

   • You are a winner because _____
     _____

   • You are a lover when you _____
     _____

   • You are a friend when _____
     _____

   • You are my hero when _____
     _____

   Read Genesis 1 out loud and in unison as a family. Then share as a family:

   • What is good about our world is _____

   • What is good about our nation is _____

   • What is good about our family is _____

Now turn to each person in your family and say this to
them: One way I see the image of God shining through
you is:

_____

_____

_____

_____

8

"Get It Together" — Finances

The primary key to getting it together in your finances is to spend less than you make! There are households earning $36,000 a year that are much happier and more fulfilled than some making $72,000 a year simply because they are living within their incomes. They aren't playing the catch-up game with the Jones, buying things they really don't need and can't afford, just to impress the people they don't like.

The Mont Blanc pen is nice, but only if you can afford the luxury of a great writing instrument. Having nice things does not make you a money-hungry materialist, although the more you accomplish materially, the more options you have available to you and the greater the susceptibility to having an "ego" problem and making the wrong choices.

Talents, good looks, ambition and any special feature you have are gifts from God. They are blessings to be thankful for, not for getting overconfident about "self." When you perform well and get compliments, you should inhale them, not swallow them. For example, someone might say to you that you've done a great job. Simply say, "Thank you, I try to do my best." The negative side to the answer is, "Oh, I was lucky, I'm really not that great" or the overconfident side answers, "Oh, it was nothing, just a piece of cake," whereas a simple thank you would be appropriate.

It has been said that the root of all unhappiness is comparison. Determine what contributes to your happiness and "Go for it." Do not let anyone steal your dreams. Protect and fight for them. These goals or dreams help you create the energy and efficiency to get into action. The larger the dreams/goals, the more planning and effort will be required to make them come true.

Happiness can be boiled down to an attitude of thanksgiving for who you are and what you have. This is opposed to envying what others have. You can never be happy if you are jealous or envy what other people have.

One of the major steps you need to take to cause your dreams to become a reality is to get control of your finances. The system I am going to share with you has worked for me. Saving money is like losing weight. There is no simple way to do it. Find something that works and stick with it.

Many years ago, I read the book, *The Richest Man in Babylon.* The book taught me the value of having your money work for you instead of always having you work for the money. This means that you have to get some money extra so that you can invest, therefore letting money be your slave. I had a good income. However, we were broke. We didn't have enough money to do all that we wanted or needed to do. Every time we tried to save from what was left after the month was over never worked, or saying when we get a raise in income we'll save, or after we pay off the car, then we'll save.

You may be like us; the savings account never happened, or if it got started, it was used for some unexpected emergency. The system I'm going to share with you will work for you, too! It will change your economic life and better prepare you for the future. But you have to have the strong will to keep the decisions made for saving final. Once you have decided to save, you must keep that money and use it only for what you have determined.

I recommend you start this with your next paycheck. I know you're broke. If you were to put 10 percent of your paycheck away into a savings account, you would not have enough money to pay your bills for this month. Well, I'm sorry to say, you're normal/average (average is defined as the best of the worst and the worst of the best). You should want to break away from the average. This is a decision you will never regret in any endeavor of your life.

To start, you'll need to set a percentage of your income away monthly to a savings/investment account. The percentage of money is the most important starting point. People have told me that they have automatic deductions from their paychecks and that's their savings program. I do not like those programs because it lets someone else do the savings for you instead of you controlling your financial future. Once you start with the percentage, it is extremely important that you stick by that percentage until you get comfortable with it and move on the ideal percentage for your goals. The ideal goal for us is 40 percent, leaving 60 percent to spend on our lifestyle.

To get started, establish a percentage of your income to go into two accounts: a savings/investment account and a donations account. Stick with the percentage you decide upon until you are comfortable with it. Then move on to the ideal percentage for your goals.

There is a progressive system of saving that you can grow with. Begin by writing two checks for the percentage you have established: one for your savings/investment account, and the other for God's account. Why God's account? To have true happiness, you can't build estates just for you and your family. You need a bigger picture of caring for other people. The first account is for your earthly success. The second is for your spiritual success and happiness. God doesn't need your money. You need to give the money so you don't get too hung up on it. That's why everything needs to be in percentages instead of in dollar amounts.

When your income goes up, even though the percentage stays the same, your savings will increase. If your monthly income is $3,000 and you have decided to start with 2.5 percent for each account, you would write two checks, each for $75. Write the checks and put them in your desk drawer. The money disappears from your regular checking account. The idea in writing the checks is to take the money out of accessibility for spending. Your checkbook can go in the hole $150 without causing a check to bounce because you have $150 worth of checks in your desk drawer.

Next month follow the same procedure and paper clip the two new checks to the first two checks. Continue this procedure until your checking account gets to a point where cashing the first set of checks will not cause any checks to bounce.

I had to go eight months before I could cash the first month's checks. My checkbook was always in the hole, but I never bounced a check because of the checks I held in my desk drawer.

When you cash the checks, set up two different accounts, as I mentioned earlier:

1. *God's account* should be a checking account so you can use it to give money to God's work. You could call this account a "donations" account.

2. *An investment account* should initially be in a regular savings account.

Each month, as finances permit, continue to write current checks and deposit previous checks that can be cashed without bouncing any checks. Though it may take time to do this, you will come to a point where you can write your checks for the current month and cash them at the same time.

When you reach this level, raise your percentage to 5 percent and repeat the same procedure. At later intervals, increase the percentage to 7.5 percent and finally to 10 percent.

As your investment money increases, put part of it into higher interest CD's and then start an investment portfolio. I started with real estate and saved $3,000 to purchase a 10-acre piece of property that I could subdivide into two parcels. I arranged my payment for the balance of the land to be within the 10 percent I was putting in my investment account each month. The time came when I did subdivide the land, sold both parcels and added several thousand dollars to my investment account. All profits should go right back into your investment money which can be used to purchase more property or to make other investments.

At some point, you may need to split up your investment portfolio so you won't have all your investment money in real estate. Don't put all of your eggs in one basket! My recommendation would be three-fourths real estate and one-fourth mutual funds.

If you are self-employed, I recommend that you open a third account for taxes and insurance. Establish a percentage to be deducted from each check according to the tax bracket you are in.

It is great fun to have money to invest that doesn't come from your regular checking account. It is also a wonderful feeling to have money in your donations account to use as you see others' needs or as God directs you.

An example of one of my investments was my dream of starting a U.S. National Bank. It was called Crown National Bank. After four years of satisfying the government regulators, we finally went to a stock sale in September of 1987. We tried earnestly for the balance of our six months to sell the stock to no avail. Finally, we had to take four and a half years of work and almost $500,000 and say good-bye to my chairmanship of Crown National Bank. It was a very sad time in our lives, but sixty days after closing the bank down, I took my wife to Paris, France, for our twentieth wedding anniversary. The money I lost in the bank adventure was from our investment account. It had nothing to do with our regular checking account. Consequently, the anniversary trip was on.

It is a wonderful feeling to have money in your donations account to use as you see the need and/or as you feel God is directing you. Prior to this system, there were several times I would like to have given more, but the money was just not in our regular checking account. By having the money put into God's account, the dollars are there, regardless of what is happening in your regular checking account. It is a real blessing to see a need or feel a special calling and have the money available to give.

Isaiah 48:17 (NKJV) says, **I am the Lord your God, Who teaches you to profit, Who leads you by the way you should go.** Deuteronomy 8:18a (NKJV) says, **And you shall remember the Lord your God, for it is He who gives you power to get wealth.**

Obviously, God is interested in helping you to get it together in your finances. He wants to lead you in the financial area of your life and teach you how to profit. His investment counsel is trustworthy!

I know this procedure will work for you. It will take discipline to write the checks each month. It will take discipline not to spend the money when your investment account increases. The benefits will financially be of such a blessing it is worth all the pain of discipline. Another benefit is the example you show your children. Delayed gratification is something that should be taught early in a person's life. You work first, then you receive. Don't get caught with a credit card every time you have a whimsical desire.

Bible Study

INSTRUCTIONS: Be honest with yourself as you complete this study. If you are studying in a group or with your family, share those things you feel most comfortable in sharing. Do one question each day for the next week, or spend thirty minutes completing the entire study at one time.

For Couples...

1. Share with one another:

   - What is easiest about giving to God?

   - What is most difficult about giving to God?

   - What does God expect of us in our giving to Him?

2. As a couple, read the following verses and explain their meaning to each other:

   - Deuteronomy 8:18a

   - Isaiah 48:17

   - Malachi 3:10-12

   - Matthew 6:19-21

   Share where you think your treasure is and what treasure you will pass on to your children in future generations as an inheritance.

For Families...

1. Have everyone in the family take a piece of paper and write down what item or thing is a family's most significant and important treasure. After everyone has written down their idea for the family treasure, share with the family what was written down and why.

2. As a family, read together Matthew 6:19-21. As a family, discuss:

   • How does our family honor God with our giving?

   • Where are the treasures of our family?

   • What are we investing in as a family and will it last forever?

3. Go around as a family and have everyone in the family share:

   • The most important treasure our family has is _____

   _____

4. Now, as a family, have a prayer of thanksgiving for your treasures.

9

"Get It Together" — Free Enterprise

We each have a role to play in preserving the freedom of our country. Today, young people with CD headsets sit on green meadows, seemingly without a care in the world, while soldiers even younger than they, have fought and died for the freedom they enjoy.

Few people have taken the time to teach the blessings we enjoy as Americans. I challenge myself, other parents and grandparents to learn and then teach the ones they love why our country is the most desirable place on earth to live.

Many immigrants who have come to our country have used the free enterprise system to become wealthy. For the first time in their lives, hard work, savings and delayed gratification are working for them. Several families often live in one home until they can afford a second one. They work long, hard hours on jobs no one else wants, and they save their money. This is exactly what our forefathers did to make America great.

We have a responsibility to teach these new Americans our past history so they too can preserve it and teach it to their future generations. In addition to teaching them "The Pledge of Allegiance," we need to make sure they understand the private enterprise system that made the pledge of protection.

The richness of America goes beyond natural resources and geographical location. It is the heart and soul of the

American spirit that makes our country great. We must not let the rural American attitude be forgotten or lost in our fast-paced lives. This, of course, starts with you and me.

You can read a portion of America's history each week to begin your historical growth. Your weekly study time is great for starting a family project about some aspect of American history. (Your local library will be able to assist you in finding materials that best explain America's history.)

We took a family trip to New England, and seeing the Freedom Trail in Boston and the battlefields of Lexington and Gettysburg did something for our personal national pride.

Why is America changing? Is it the fast pace of life, alcohol, drugs, self-centeredness, or a combination of all of these? My belief is that we, as a nation, have over-regulated ourselves to the point the American spirit has been changed to a job mentality instead of an entrepreneur mentality.

At the turn of the 19th century, 90 percent of us worked for ourselves. Today, 90 percent of Americans work for someone else. The emphasis of much of the college teaching today is on how to be good employees rather than building great minds to develop new products, new fields and better ways of doing things.

One mentality that is prevalent too often today is, "Somebody owes me something," instead of using the God-given talents and abilities to lead them to their ambition.

When 90 percent of Americans worked for themselves, they were typically farmers and small business people. In those days, their farm crops were their livelihood. When crops failed, it caused extreme hardship, but the people found a way to handle it.

Political offices were held as a way of giving back to the country that supported them. Today's politicians hold office as a way of getting opportunities. There was community involvement to help neighbors and fellow church members as opposed to the "handouts" we have in today's society.

This means we no longer have 90 percent of the people making their own decisions and being accountable for their economic success from direct ownership. Consequently, we have developed a paycheck mentality. That mentality can regress to, "I don't care who pays the check as long as I get a check." This is very dangerous thinking, because total accountability for your financial sustenance is placed in someone else's hands.

Our recommendations to get it together in free enterprise are:

1. *Become informed.* Study to gain a better understanding of what makes America great. Purpose to learn more about your local, state and federal governments.

2. *Become involved.* This can be done by voting, helping a candidate of your choice and giving financial support. Don't be an island of non-involvement.

3. *Appreciate history.* Appreciate who and what propelled America to greatness. Don't be too quick to condemn the motives of others until you have evaluated your own! You won't have to read very much American history to discover that most of those we consider "great Americans" were common people who dared to pursue God-motivated goals for the good of everyone. Their vision went beyond "us four and no more."

4. *Start your own business.* Many opportunities exist for starting your own business. In many cases, you can start part time and work your way up the ladder of success until you can be involved full time.

The first step you need to take is to examine your possibilities. What assets and talents do you possess? How can you market these assets and talents?

I dare you: Make free enterprise work for you! You can do it!

I can do everything

through him

who gives me strength.

Philippians 4:13

P.S. to learn more about our history, I would recommend two videos.

1) Foundation for American Government, and

2) America's Godly Heritage.

These can be purchased from Dave Barton of Wall Guilders, P.O. Box 397, Aledo, TX 76008, 817-441-6044.

Bible Study

INSTRUCTIONS: Be honest with yourself as you complete this study. If you are studying in a group or with your family, share those things you feel most comfortable in sharing. Do one question each day for the next week, or spend thirty minutes completing the entire study at one time.

For Couples...

1. As a couple, share some of the business dreams and ideas that you have.

2. Together pray for God's wisdom and direction, and then say together in unison, **"I can do all things through Jesus Christ Who gives me strength"** (Phil. 4:13).

3. What are some of the ways you can teach the free enterprise system to your children?

For Families...

1. As a family, have a discussion about what the free enterprise system is all about in America.

2. Ask each person in the family to share some of the dreams that he/she has about starting a business.

3. Discuss any plans that you have as a family of starting your own business together and involving everyone in the family. On a piece of paper, list the possibilities and the reasons why you might start your own business as a family.

4. As a family, say together in unison, **"We can do all things through Christ Who gives us strength"** (Phil. 4:13).

10

"Get It Together" — Together

When I started this book, I had no idea how I would end it, but now it is clear: True commitment will carry you through from what looks like total defeat to God's highest and best victory! I know!

When my wife and I said our wedding vows in July, 1968, our commitment was "in sickness and in health, till death do us part." Sharon made that commitment to me, and I made that commitment to her. The finale was, "The two shall become one flesh. What God has joined together, let no man separate."

Three weeks after our marriage, Sharon's ankles swelled to twice their original size. At first we thought it was due to the excitement of the wedding, setting up our own apartment, or the anxiety of being on our own for the very first time.

After two weeks with no change in the swelling, we went to the doctor. To our surprise, Sharon had developed a rare kidney disease called Glumeral Nephritis. It was believed that chronic renal failure eventually would stop the kidney function completely. At that time, kidney transplants were uncommon, and dialysis was in its developmental stages.

After three weeks of marriage, we moved in with my parents so Sharon would have 24-hour supervision of her kidney functions. She was started on a variety of medications. We were so blessed to have parents who were willing to help us through this difficult time. Many of us tend to forget how much our parents have done for us and how much they mean to us. (Why not give your parents a call right now and just say "thank you"?)

The doctors recommended that we not have any children during this time, because they didn't feel a baby would survive the nine-month pregnancy, plus Sharon would be at great risk. We did not have any children until we were awarded a trip to St. Thomas in the Virgin Islands on the yacht "Enterprise." What was not planned happened, and Sharon became pregnant.

Doctors recommended that we abort the baby to protect Sharon's life. For a young married man, this was quite a decision. I wanted to protect my young wife against the overwhelming odds of tragedy, but the thought of ending a new baby's life so drastically was very difficult. The dilemma was solved when Sharon said, "Dennis, I cannot abort this baby and live with myself. I have to trust God and see what our future and our baby's future has in store. I would rather die giving birth than to take this precious one's life."

The nine-month challenge (and blessing) began! Sharon had to quit smoking. (Today, it's hard to believe that we ever smoked!) During this time Sharon was allowed no pain relievers and no weight gain. Each pound she gained meant a greater risk to the baby. I was so proud of her because she only gained one and a half pounds during the entire pregnancy.

We were blessed with many great friends. One of them, June Clayton, a mother of four, stayed overnight one evening to count the minutes between contractions. She helped to calm our anxieties.

On October 3, 1973, Annette was born. Sharon sent me out of the room when the contractions were too much for her to bear. She instructed me to tell the waiting relatives that everything was going great. When we went into the delivery room, I was in control and everything was fine until the doctor said, "It looks like you have a pretty normal little girl — ten fingers and ten toes."

That sent me to the floor! I remember hearing the doctor say, "Nurse, get the Dad!" I never thought of the possibility that my child wouldn't have ten fingers and ten toes. I just knew we were so blessed that the reality of the moment got to me!

It is so fulfilling to follow God's Word, allowing it to be your guide. It takes the pressure off of making decisions by yourself. Not only were we blessed with a precious daughter, but the degradation of Sharon's kidneys slowed. When a woman becomes pregnant and has a baby, her body chemistry changes. That change, we believe, created a reaction in the kidneys that slowed the disease down so that the failure point was put farther into the future, 25 years to be exact!

Two years after Annette was born, Sharon became pregnant with our second child, Dennis, Jr. Again, we went through the challenging nine months, watching the effects on the kidneys, with restrictions of no weight gain and no pain relievers.

When Dennis, Jr. arrived, Sharon's response was, "I just can't believe it's a boy!" Now our family was complete.

After Dennis, Jr.'s birth, the doctors recommended that we have no more children because the strain on Sharon's kidneys during pregnancy was too much of a risk. We knew we should not have any more children, even though Sharon originally wanted thirteen!

With the help of natural vitamins, exercise and hard work, our lives were normal. Sometimes we worked too hard to notice. Not knowing how long my wife would live gave me a sense of tolerance and urgency. Tolerance in not allowing little things bug me, yet a sense of urgency because in the back of my mind was the continual question, "What if?"

Husbands and wives, develop a tolerance with each other, because you really don't know how long you will have each other. Just because there is no serious illness over your head doesn't mean you are guaranteed a long life together.

In January, 1994, it became evident that Sharon would soon be on kidney dialysis. At that time she underwent surgery to have an access made in her arm for the process of dialysis to flow through, called a fistula. The doctor spliced a vain and an artery together to allow the flow to happen. We called it "a river runs through it," because that's exactly what it felt like. The healing process was to take at least two months, and that was exactly the time Sharon had before she needed to start dialysis.

I have shared all this with you to tell you the conclusion of the old life and the beginning of the new for Sharon and me. On March 22, 1994, Sharon's kidneys finally quit filtering the blood well enough for her to live without kidney dialysis, where you are hooked up to a machine which takes over the function of your kidneys. During this process, the blood comes out of the body, it is cleansed and then it is put back into the body.

I would like to take this opportunity to thank all the people who work in dialysis centers across the country for their care, concern and willingness to serve people at such a challenging time in their lives. I am partial to Evergreen Dialysis in San Jose, our home base, and to Chattanooga, Tennessee, where we met some great people.

Sharon had been on dialysis three days a week for two weeks when a very precious friend, Sherry Gilson, called to tell her that the Lord had prompted her to tell Sharon about a special service at her church that evening. Sharon had been to church that morning and was extremely tired, but she felt that if she was supposed to go, when she mentioned it to her sister, Cleta, she would respond positively.

Cleta was overwhelmingly excited about the service, so they went. The elders prayed over Sharon and she was out for about a half hour. When she awoke, she felt great.

The next time Sharon went to the doctor he told her that her kidneys had kicked in and that she only needed dialysis two days a week. Praise the Lord! That was one less day to be stuck with needles and one less day to be at the center for five hours.

This was a difficult time for us, but compared to the alternative of death, it was great. Sometimes people with challenges only look at the challenge. Analyze your alternatives, and I believe you will be grateful for what is available to you.

Once on dialysis we began to look for other options. Because of Sharon's age and health, she became a candidate for a kidney transplant. She was put on the donor's list, with an estimated one to two years of waiting.

At Stanford Medical Clinic during Sharon's explanation of options for the future, Jane Waskerwitz, a sweet lady, asked if I wanted to be tested to see if by some chance I was compatible with Sharon. It is extremely unusual for unrelated people to match. By having the surgery, we would become the first husband-wife donor-recipient combination in Standord history. To the clinic's surprise, my tissue matched and our blood types were compatible. The next question was, "Would I be willing to donate my kidney?"

My decision was made 26 years earlier when we were married. When I said, "I do," I meant "I do." When we said our marriage vows, we became one flesh in Christ.

> Husbands, love your wives, just as Christ loved the church and gave himself up for her
>
> To make her holy, cleansing her by the washing with water through the word,
>
> And to present her to himself as a radiant church, without stain or wrinkle or any other blemish, but holy and blameless.
>
> In this same way, husbands ought to love their wives as their own bodies. He who loves his wife loves himself.
>
> After all, no one ever hated his own body, but he feeds and cares for it, just as Christ does the church.
>
> Ephesians 5:25-29

I must admit, however, that I had my moments! When they explained about the catheter for my urine flow after the surgery, my heart beat a little faster! I am a very private person and real sensitive when it comes to that part of my anatomy! Sharon listened and watched as the doctor explained it to me. Watching my eyes, she was almost convinced that she had just lost her best kidney option!! Then I said, "Don't explain anymore. My decision is 'yes,' and nothing is going to change it. We will live and deal with whatever happens."

I did think of Jesus in the Garden of Gethsemane when He prayed to God before the crucifixion. **"Abba, Father," he said, "everything is possible for you. Take this cup from me. Yet not what I will, but what you will"** (Mark 14:36). I understood the significance of that prayer when I asked, "God, is there some other way?"

Time was short because Sharon's health was degenerating and the fistula had collapsed. Doctors placed an access in her neck, and she was told it would only last two to four weeks. Then she would have to undergo another surgery to create an access in her leg. The kidney transplant was completed before additional surgery was necessary.

The operation was scheduled for August 17, 1994. I scheduled a business presentation for the evening of the 16th, not knowing I would have to go into the hospital the day before for more tests and X-rays to decide which kidney would be taken from me.

Before I share about the surgeries, I want to take this opportunity to give my recommendation for Stanford University Medical Center, Stanford Hospital and the multi-organ transplant team, directed by Donald C. Dafoe, M.D., transplant surgeon. We are indeed grateful for their excellent standards and performance during this process.

Dr. Dafoe has put together a tremendous staff, including my surgeon, Dr. Edward J. Alfrey, and Sharon's surgeon, Dr. Paul Kuo. With the supervision of Dr. Dafoe, the care of all the staff, including the transplant coordinators, the hospital staff, the Medical Center staff, and especially the transplant center principals, was of highest quality.

Two other interim team members we would like to thank are Dr. Annette Cholon and Dr. Abe Deanda, both resident doctors. It is so interesting how God works. Drs. Cholon and Deanda worked with the transplant team for a short time. Annette covered for someone who was ill at the time, and Abe was basically doing his time in the transplant area, as he was required to do in all areas of the hospital. Annette assisted with my surgery, and Abe assisted with Sharon's. They are two very dedicated people, and I believe they will continue to do great things in whatever field of medicine they choose. We thank God that He placed them with us at this particular time.

Sharon and I have always tried to follow God's Word and His will for our lives. However, some decisions are not as clear as others. Sometimes we must step out in faith. In our case, the decision was clear.

Prayers by thousands of our friends guided the surgeons' hands to perform perfectly. From the time my kidney arrived in Sharon's operating room, it took only nineteen minutes until kidney transplant completion, Incidentally, this is a record for Stanford. Typically, it takes from one to two days for the kidney to begin to function. My kidney began to function in Sharon within one minute after it was attached. Needless to say, it was a little more difficult to insert the catheter.

Abe, the resident doctor, told Sharon a couple of days later that when they opened her up and placed the kidney in her, the hole where it was to go was the perfect size. He said it was as though the opening was designed especially for my kidney to be placed there. This space, we believe, was designed by God to hold the kidney perfectly!

Sharon's surgery went great. I had never had any type of surgery in my entire life, nor had I ever taken any drugs, with the exception of aspirin. My body went bonkers with the epidural! It was actually the worst case of reaction to anesthesia that Stanford had seen in a donor in two years.

Once I started to recover from the anesthesia, which took two and a half days (each minute seemed like ten minutes and ten minutes seemed like an hour), then my body reacted to the pain relievers for another two and a half days. The pain, nausea, vomiting and discomfort of the five days finally spoke to me. I was out of control. I could not handle the situation alone. No food for five days, along with everything else, wore my resistance and strength down to the bottom!

When you are at the lowest time in your life, you realize how empty your life would be without Jesus, regardless of how much you have accomplished in the natural. Though I had accepted Christ as my Savior many years before, I finally had to relent to the awesome power of Jesus. No more controlling it myself, no more trying to do it by myself.

At 4:36 a.m. on August 22, 1994, I had reached bottom and I admitted, "Lord, I can't handle this anymore." Suddenly, I felt a peace come over me as the gentle words of Jesus came to me: **Never will I leave you; never will I forsake you** (Heb. 13:5).

At that point, I felt so close to my Lord Jesus Christ. I can't explain the feeling. Though Jesus had been my Savior, at that moment He became my buddy. I felt everything was okay. I started crying and continued to cry for an hour just praising God.

Later that morning as I tried to explain to Sharon what had happened to me, I couldn't get the words out without crying again. Even today, as I continue to grow healthier every day and my life is back to a faster pace, my eyes still tear up as I remember that special moment.

By the next day I was feeling so much better that we were released to finish our recovery at home. The blessing I received from giving equals Sharon's blessing from receiving!

What a thrill to see Sharon be able to eat almost anything, within reason, again. Her skin is now pink instead of yellow, and she feels good for the first time in years.

Through all of this, our families played a significant part. Sharon's parents came to stay with us for a month after the surgery to take care of us and drive us wherever we needed to go. My parents were at the hospital constantly and then helped throughout the next month and beyond.

My brothers and sister were an answer to prayer. I will always treasure Frank and his wife Barbara, David and his wife Sherree and Debbie and her husband Phil. Their involvement and support were priceless. Even our nieces and nephews played a big part in our healing. Sharon's sister Cleta was unable to be with us following the surgeries, but she came to be with Sharon to prepare her for the surgery. We felt her prayer support.

Mark and Sandy Day have come to be a part of our family in a very special way. They were with us the weekend before surgery for a business function and asked to stay through the surgery to pray. They spent a week with us and were a tremendous support. We couldn't love them more if they were our own children. Mark gave the most vivid picture of *commitment* when he told us later that he watched Sharon say "I love you" to me as I was being taken to surgery. Then I told her "I love you" as I left for the operating room with thumbs up!

Our Eternal Commitment

When Sharon and I were married, we had no idea how God would use this situation to touch our lives and the lives of others. Sharon has often said that, had she known about the kidney disease before we were married, she would not have married me.

God knows each of us intimately. He made the disease common knowledge three weeks *after* we were married. God's timing, of course, is always perfect. Thank You, God, that we can always count on Your perfection!

Because of our perfect God, we have two wonderful children, Annette and Dennis, Jr. Probably another chapter could be written on how it feels at twenty and eighteen to watch both of your parents being wheeled into operating rooms at the same time, plus knowing your parents spent time with their attorney before the surgeries to make sure that all their legal details were up to date.

God's mercy was evident in many ways through our surgeries, and especially through our children. We have received many cards and letters thanking us for their prompt calls via Amvox. They kept everyone updated every few hours so that our friends would know the status of our progress and how to pray. Dennis, Jr. continued to take care of our office, and Annette was a tremendous support, even though she was preparing to leave for her senior year at George Fox College three days later.

To whom and to what are *you* committed? Now is the time to commit your life to the one true, loving God — the God Who formed you in your mother's womb; the God Who, even when you are not searching for Him, is searching for you; the God Who, when you are in the deepest pit, will be the lifter of your head and will set your feet on solid ground!

We are excited about what the future holds for us and for our children as well. Had we not committed our lives to God and then to each other, there would have been no children. Because of our commitment, however, God has been able to work through us to touch the lives of others. God is working through our children to touch others. He wants to work through you, too. Your commitment to Him opens the door to His guidance and blessings.

This book began with God and it ends with God! Today can be a new start for you towards the rest of your life. Now is the time to GET IT TOGETHER...TOGETHER!!

Bible Study

INSTRUCTIONS: Be honest with yourself as you complete this study. If you are studying in a group or with your family, share those things you feel most comfortable in sharing. Do one question each day for the next week, or spend thirty minutes completing the entire study at one time.

1. Are there things you would like to say good-bye to in your old life so you can welcome the new life God has destined for you? What are some of the things you want to say good-bye to?

   a. _____

   b. _____

   c. _____

   d. _____

   e. _____

2. Habakkuk 2:2,3 (NKJV) says, **Write the vision and make it plain on tablets, that he may run who reads it. For the vision is yet for an appointed time; but at the end it will speak, and it will not lie. Though it tarries, wait for it; because it will surely come, it will not tarry.**

   Write the vision God has spoken for you to fulfill:

   _____

   _____

   _____

   _____

   _____

   _____

   _____

   _____

_____

_____

_____

3. Isaiah 43:18,19 says:

    "Forget the _____ things; do not dwell on
    the past. See, I am doing a _____ _____! Now
    it springs up; do you not perceive it? I am making a way
    in the desert and streams in the wasteland."

4. You must have a servant's heart to fulfill God's destiny
    for you. Matthew 20:26-28 says:

    "...Whoever wants to become great among you must be
    your_____, and whoever wants to
    be first must be your _____ [servant] — Just
    as the Son of Man did not come to be served, but to
    _____, and to give his life as a ransom for
    many."

5. Hebrews 12:2 says, "Let us fix our eyes on_____,
    the author and perfecter of our faith...." To fix your eyes
    on the challenge always causes it to become bigger. To
    fix your eyes on Jesus is to fix your eyes upon the
    Answer to your every need!

6. Mark 9:23 holds a great promise for you: "Everything is
    possible for him who _____."

7. Proverbs 3:5,6 gives you a key to receiving God's direc-
    tion:

    "_____ in the Lord with all your heart
    and_____ _____ on your own under-
    standing; in all your ways _____
    him, and he will make your paths straight."

8. Regardless of the challenges you are facing at the mo-
    ment, God gives you an unchanging promise in Psalm

34:19:

"A righteous man [or woman] may have many troubles, but the Lord delivers him [or her] from them _____."

9. Psalm 3:3 says God is a _____ to you. He bestows_____on you and _____ your head! Hallelujah! He never changes!! (Heb. 13:8).